WHAT IN
HELL
DO YOU
WANT?

JESSE DUPLANTIS

What In Hell Do You Want?
ISBN 0-9728712-8-4
Copyright © 2003 by Jesse Duplantis

Published by Jesse Duplantis Ministries
P. O. Box 20149
New Orleans, Louisiana 70141
www.jdm.org

Contents

CHAPTER 1

What In Hell Do You Want?

Sin will take you further than you want to go. It will keep you longer than you want to stay and charge you more than you want to pay. Sin won't ask for too much in the beginning, but in the end, it will steal everything you've got.

Many years ago, I was at the home of a preacher and he was talking to me about his many problems. He was considering quitting God, the ministry and going back into his old sinful lifestyle. After a long explanation, he said, "You know, I just can't live for God anymore." I looked at him and asked, "What in *Hell* do you want?"

He looked at me with shock and said, "Oh, Brother Jesse! You're cussing!"

"No," I said, "I'm not cussing. That is your stinking mind. I want to know what in *Hell* you want?" He didn't know what to say. So, I grabbed him by the wrist and did something that probably seemed crazy. I said, "Come here!" I jerked him out of his seat, walked him to the kitchen and turned on the gas stove. As the fire shot up, I held his hand above the flame. I didn't put his hand in the fire, but I made sure to hold his hand just above it so he could feel the heat.

"Do you feel this?" I hollered, "Feel it? Do you enjoy this?" He looked at me like I was nuts and started trying to wiggle his hand out of my grip. I held him there for just a second or so more and kept asking him, "Do you *like* it? Does *it* like you?" Then, I released his hand and questioned him again.

"Did you *enjoy* the flame? Did it bless you?"

"NO!" he hollered back at me indignantly.

"Well, it is heat like that that's going to burn your whole body for eternity if you choose Hell."

Now, some people might call that crazy, but at the time, I eyed the stove and that was the only thing that popped into my head to do, so I did it! I'll admit that I probably wouldn't do that today! I'm older and wiser, but this man was a friend. I cared about him. I didn't want the devil to steal his life and ministry. Bottom line, he needed a wake-up call! He had allowed discouragement to fester in his mind for so long that it clouded his view of reality.

Although he knew the truth, this pastor was about to leave his church and abandon the people that God had placed in his care. He was about to start down a road that could only lead to disappointment, confusion and misery for himself, his family and his congregation.

What would make him give up a life of serving God? Disappointment? No. Discouragement? No. Discontentment? Not really. There is only one thing that can make a person reject Jesus and choose a life of sin – *Deception*.

This pastor had deceived himself into thinking that life was better without God and that nothing he did mattered anymore. He thought his life was useless and his work was fruitless; that nobody really needed him and he didn't need anybody.

What was the devil dangling in front of his face? The deceptive notion that, without God, his life would be easy and trouble-free. The pastor considered the notion and was tempted to give up on the whole ball of wax. Now, giving up is one temptation that has hit home with just about everyone at one time or another.

I'm glad the pastor trusted me enough to talk to me about what was going on. Not many men are able to say, "Hey, I'm having trouble with this." It's an honorable man who will come clean to a friend. I admit, I can be unorthodox in my way of getting a point across, but I knew that the man was listening to lies from the pit of Hell and I figured that *he* needed to know it too.

The bottom line is that this pastor didn't understand the repercussions of the choice that he was about to make. After years of living for God, he had become so familiar with the things of God, so comfortable with his ho-hum Christian walk and so accustomed to his lifestyle that he honestly didn't understand what kind of "fire" he was playing with.

I honestly believe that this man needed to not only *hear* what I had to say, but he needed to *feel* the heat! He needed to know that he was about to throw away a good future with both hands. He needed to wake up to deception and stop toying with a lifestyle that was going to steal, kill and destroy his life. And, well, at that time in my life, I was just crazy enough to give him a fiery illustration he wouldn't soon forget!

The Temptation to Give Up

Even the disciples of Jesus Christ felt hopeless and useless and wanted to give up from time to time. After Jesus was crucified on the cross, the disciples lost all hope. In John 21:3, Peter said, *"I go a fishing..."* and got a load of converts saying, *"We go also with thee!"* They thought the ministry was over. They gave up and went back to their old jobs. So, everyone has felt like giving up at one time or another – and many people *have* given up.

But, notice, the disciples didn't give up for good. They didn't spend the rest of their lives fishing. No, they got back up again. They shook off the dust, turned back to God, received power and went on to change the world with the message of Jesus Christ.

No matter where you are today, God can use you. He can open your eyes to what is exactly causing you to stumble and give you the strength to resist the devil – no matter what he's trying to hurt you with.

God will help you, if you let Him. He'll help *anyone* who turns to Him. Remember that Jesus had a staff of twelve that most people would have fired the first week! Peter would cut you, cuss at you and then pray for you. Judas was stealing money, John was always laying his head on Jesus' chest and Thomas didn't believe half of what He said! Yet, Jesus stuck it out with them.

Even though they were misfits, Jesus taught them, empowered them and then, set them loose on the earth with a mission to win souls and share His teachings with others. Just reading about all the crazy things the disciples did in the Bible ought to prove to you that God is super-patient. He's super-longsuffering! He can help anybody, including you.

So, you see, God is always there for you. When you're threatening to give up on Him and life, He's there. When you want to hit your mother-in-law, He's there too! When you're so distraught that you don't know what to do and you're bawling and squalling and having a pity party of one, He's there waiting for you to turn to Him and do what His Word says so that He can help you straighten out the crooked paths of your life.

God loves you and He's not looking for ways to send you to the fiery pit. He's searching for ways to reach your heart – to help you – so that you live well on this earth and in the afterlife. God loved the disciples and He knew their human frailty. He knows your human frailty too. It's time for you to start seeing through the devil's lies because, once you start doing that, victory is on the way!

It's About More Than Hell; It's About Avoiding a Hellish Life

As you may know, I'm an evangelist and if you've heard much of my preaching, you'll know that I don't focus on the end times or the book of Revelation very much. I consider my primary calling to spread the joy of the Lord and the news of salvation through Jesus Christ. As I always say, "If you get your soul in order now, you won't have to worry about what happens later!"

But, Hell is a very real place, and according to the Bible, if you choose to ignore or reject the Lord, you're going to end up where the devil is destined to end up – in Hell, dealing with a bad choice for all of eternity. As an evangelist, my calling is to shine the light of the Word so that it exposes the devil's lies. I do my best to speak and write as plainly as I know how so that everyone can understand how important it is to make the wise choice to accept the Lord.

You see, living for God is about more than just avoiding Hell after death. It's about avoiding a hellish life right here on earth. If you turn to God and start living according to the teachings of His

Word, you'll be on your way to a good life here and an even better life in Heaven.

Any trouble you'll have to deal with day-to-day is only temporary, and as you rely on God and your faith, that trouble is actually changeable. You can turn the tables on the devil and send his old, ugly self running for cover! You see, God gave you His Word and sent you His Son so that you could have a powerful substance called faith.

There is nothing more success-producing than the faith of God. And, that empowering substance called *faith* begins working in your life when you choose to live for eternity with God…when you choose to say, "There is *nothing* in Hell that I want!"

Heaven – A Better Place

Hell is hot. The more I've researched the place, the more I know that there is nothing in Hell that I want either – not one stinking, little thing. But, the more I read about Heaven, the more I know that I want everything that God has for me. Heaven isn't hot and miserable; it's cool and refreshing. It's beautiful. There is no night in Heaven and no need for sleep either. You feel perfectly rested at all times.

In Heaven, there are no hospitals and thank God, no taxes! There will be no struggling or stress, no aggravation or worry. It's like the best day you ever had multiplied by a million. Think about that. The streets are pure gold. I want to slide down those streets in my socks!

The Bible tells us that Heaven's gate is made out of pearl – not a bunch of pearls but one pearl. Man, I wonder what the size of the oyster must be?! Do you realize what Cajuns like me are going to do with a big oyster like that? We'll be slapping Tabasco sauce on that baby and sucking on it for eternity!

What in Heaven do we want? We want fellowship! We want good times! In Heaven, there'll be no locks on the doors. There won't be any fights and no church splits. Everybody will be enjoying the days and nobody will be comparing themselves to each other. There'll be no envy or jealousy. There will be no prejudice and no strife. Everywhere we will go, we will smell the fragrance of God. We will see the angels of the Lord. They will be our servants and our friends.

You may have a hard time stretching your mind to understand the concept of Heaven. It may not sound like "reality" based thinking to you, but if that's the case, it's only because you are so accustomed to living in a sin-run earth. This place is over-run with problems! Heaven is a real place and it's going to be wonderful. To know that you're going to spend eternity with God is comforting. To know that you have a friend and a Father in the Creator is just the best!

Today, we may live in a dark, sin-filled and hate-driven world, but we can *still* live good lives. We can still enjoy ourselves and get through the hard times with our faith. I believe that as Christians, we can live a godly, holy life and *not* be weird. We can live pure and feel good about it.

I believe in living holy. Some people think that holiness is about how you look – what kind of clothes you wear or what kind of clothes you won't wear – but, to me, holiness is a discipline and simply part of God's nature. When you make a choice to live for God, you're living better than anybody who has rejected Him.

You've got answers and help when you need it, and that kind of divine assistance can only help you. It's what changes you and makes others stand up and take notice.

I Was Voted "Most Changed"

When I went to my twenty-year class reunion, I was voted "Most Changed." I guess so! The person they knew was a heathen dog going to Hell! Before I made a decision to serve Christ, I lived according to my own set of rules, which was "no rules." I did what I wanted, when I wanted and had no conscience about it. I drank hard, drugged up my body and slept with whomever I wanted to sleep with. I didn't care about God and I sure didn't care about other people. The only person I really loved was me!

Then, God came into my life and everything changed. Today, I'm a preacher of the Gospel, and that is something that I never imagined that I would be. Nobody thought I'd darken the doors of a church, much less become a preacher…but God has a sense of humor and here I am. Since 1978, I've been traveling and preaching all over the U.S. and the world telling others about Jesus Christ. My life *is* the ministry and I'm constantly on-the-go.

When people notice how much I travel, they often ask me, "Why do you preach so much?" When you get down to it, what they really want to know is why I'm so enthusiastic about my salvation and sharing it with others. Well, I'm a dead man! It's no longer me who lives but God who lives in me. I chose to be spiritually "crucified" with Christ the day I recognized my need for God and His plan of redemption through Jesus Christ. That day, I decided that my life was nothing without God. It didn't matter how much money I made or how much I accomplished – without God, I was living low.

I'm a Dead Man!

So, I chose to let God into my life and started to adopt the Apostle Paul's words as my own: *"I am crucified with Christ: nevertheless I live; yet not I, but Christ liveth in me: and the life which I now live in the flesh I live by the faith of the Son of God, who loved me, and gave Himself for me. I do not frustrate the grace of God: for if righteousness come by the law, then Christ is dead in vain"* (Galatians 2:20-21).

My "God day" was the moment I surrendered to God. Now, I didn't become perfect in an instant, but I was forgiven and accepted in an instant. Instantly, when I sincerely called out to God and opened my heart to Him, He came in to save me. That was on Labor Day weekend in 1974, and it was the turning point of my life. The very moment I said, "Jesus come into my life," He heard me and saved me. What was I "saved" from? A life that was sending me to Hell, death and the grave – and, of course, the greatest thing He saved me from was myself.

That Labor Day weekend, I made a quality decision to follow God and I took my first step towards living the "crucified" life of Galatians 2:20-21. It wasn't lip service for me; it was a heart change. It was about letting Him live through me, and I've been doing that day by day ever since.

Living By the Faith of Jesus

Today, every time I do the right thing and every time I choose the right path, I'm letting more of Jesus live through me. Every time I let His Word come out of my mouth and every time I act on His Word in faith, I'm letting more of Jesus live through me.

How do I do it? The same way Paul did it: *"...by the faith of the Son of God."* Without faith, it's impossible. But, notice that it's God's faith that I use, not my own. Any faith I have comes from Him. Why do I choose to obey Him? Because He is the One *"who loved me, and gave Himself for me."* I'm grateful to Him.

I don't want to do the same wrong things over and over again. Why? Because, like the Apostle Paul, I don't want to *"frustrate the grace of God."* I want to honor God not just with my words or my intentions, but with my life. He's worth it. He gave me His best (Jesus), so I want to give Him my best. There's a better life in God for me.

Reality Check: "What In Hell Do I Want?"

So, when the devil tries to throw temptation my way, I give myself a reality check and ask myself, "What in Hell Do I Want?!" My answer is always "NOTHING!" There is nothing that the devil has to offer me that is better than God. His offer may look good, but it's not good. The grass may be green, but it's sitting over a sewer! If it's not from God, it can seem pretty on the outside, but it's rotten!

When temptation is knocking at the backdoor, not too many

people want to stop for a moment and think the situation through, but that is exactly what needs to happen. It's the only way to stop yourself from immediately obeying an impulse. If you want to do the right thing, then it takes *thought*.

Crucifying your flesh daily, instead of just on Sunday or other church days, keeps you on the right track. The Bible uses the word "sanctification" to describe the state of purity we strive for. It doesn't come by perfecting ourselves, but it comes by allowing the perfect nature of Christ to flow through us; to live *in* us and *through* us.

CHAPTER 2

The Devil is an Idiot and His Final Destination is Hell

God isn't sharing Heaven with the devil, so you can't bring his old sin there and expect to get in. You have to get rid of it by asking Jesus to come into your life. You see, God kicked the devil out of Heaven a long time ago and it doesn't look like the boy is going to be allowed to move back. God has some hot, waterfront property reserved for that fool.

> And the devil that deceived them was **cast into the lake of fire** and brimstone, where the beast and the false prophet are, and shall be tormented day and night for ever and ever.
>
> Revelations 20:10

I'm going to shout the day God relocates the devil to the lake of fire. That day is going to be divine payback for all the killing, stealing, and destroying the devil has done in the lives of people throughout the ages.

The Bible says that we're going to watch the devil get kicked into the lake of fire. I can hardly wait. I hope God lets me kick him once before he sends the boy sailing into the flames! I want to get my shot in!

It's sad to say, but the truth is that the devil won't be alone as he's sailing into the lake. The Bible says that he'll be joined by all his legions of demons, death itself and every human being who rejected Jesus and whose name is not in the Lamb's Book of Life. (See Revelations 19:20; 20:10, 14-15; 21:8) That is serious business, but it's nothing you have to worry about if you have chosen to follow Christ. It's definitely something to consider, however, if you've rejected Christ up to this point.

People like to crack jokes about Hell. They say, "Who cares? All my friends will be there with me!" But, nobody, and I do mean *nobody*, is going to be laughing when they're actually faced with the reality of Hell.

Nobody likes Hell, not even the devil. The scripture doesn't say he's going to voluntarily step in the lake and say, "Yeah, I like this place!" No, the Bible says he will be "cast" into the fiery lake. That doesn't sound like somebody who is looking forward to the flames to me. God is going to have to get the angels to throw him into the fire because, even though the devil is an idiot, he won't give in without a fight.

Don't Gamble With Eternity

I live in South Louisiana; I was born and raised here and although you may never have lived here yourself, I can personally assure you that the place exists.

Some people don't believe in Hell, but that doesn't really change anything. The place exists. Throughout the Bible, there are references to it, in straight-up teachings, warnings and in parables told by Jesus Christ. God has reiterated the idea of Hell through His prophets in the Bible, through Jesus Christ and through the apostles. As far as the Bible is concerned, it exists whether we believe or not.

Now, I'm not a debating man. Jesus never begged people to believe He was the Son of God. He never said, "Come on, I am the Son of God, really I am!" So, I'm not going to waste my time begging anyone to believe that Hell is real. If you believe the Word, I think you're wise. If you don't believe it, then go ahead and shoot the dice.

Personally, I'm not gambling with eternity! I believe the Word is true and I want to be on the winning side – the heavenly side. That's why I accepted Jesus as my Savior. I knew I was headed to Hell, but at the time, I just didn't care.

When I allowed myself to face reality, I realized that I needed God. Heaven became my reward, but it certainly isn't the only reason I chose to follow God. I knew that I needed God's love and His guidance in this life. I couldn't live on my own and have joy. I needed what God could provide – here and now, as well as in the afterlife.

People have asked me, "Well, what if you die and there is no Heaven or Hell?" My answer is simple. If everything I believe isn't true, then I'll still be glad I lived this way. After all, what have I lost? Alcoholism? Drug addiction? Misery? Hate? Raging anger? Great! I'm glad that's out of my life and I have only Jesus to thank.

Today, I live an adventurous, joyful and faith-filled life. I'm helping others to have joy and know God's principles for themselves so that they can live this life well. That's a good life to me. I like real Christianity – not the theological wilderness of religion – because it is more than just the *right* way to live. It's also a very good way to live.

Since I turned my life over to God, my life has become better and better. God has revealed His Word as truth to me time and time again. It just plain works! The more I put my faith in Him, the more He helps me. The more I apply what He teaches in His Word, the more blessed, healthy and happy my life has become.

Hell Was Created for Fallen Angels

Do you know that Hell was never created for human beings? That's why it's such a horrific place. It was created to handle outlaw angels. You see, because we know from the Word that some angels were chained in Hell for rebelling with the devil against God in Heaven, we know that Hell was in existence long before man was ever created. (See 2 Peter 2:4; Jude 1:6)

The Bible says Hell is a place where *"their worm does not die and the fire is not quenched"* (Mark 9:46-48). Jesus called it a place of *"outer darkness"* where there is a *"furnace of fire."* He said that in Hell there would be great *"wailing, weeping and gnashing of teeth."* (See Matthew 8:12; Matthew 13:42,50; Matthew 22:13; Matthew 24:51; Matthew 25:30; Luke 13:28)

As if that's not bad enough, the place is crawling with hypocrites!

> *The lord of that servant shall come in a day when he*
> *looketh not for him, and in an hour that he is not aware of,*
> *And shall cut him asunder, **and appoint him his***
> ***portion with the hypocrites:** there shall be weeping and*
> *gnashing of teeth.*
>
> Matthew 24:50-51

Can you think about all the people you can't stand? Guess what? If you choose Hell you're going to have to live with them for eternity! That alone ought to make you say, "Help me, Jesus!"

Don't Let the Devil Lie to You

The devil has been lying his fool head off since his insurrection in Heaven. He lied in Heaven to some of the angels and when we came on the scene, he started lying to us.

The devil has been continually battering mankind with the lie that you can't be happy obeying God. That's a load of junk! I obey God and I'm happy. So do millions of other believers. But, the devil sold that lie to mankind in the Garden of Eden and he's still trying to peddle that same lie to people today. Sadly, lots of people take his bait.

Freedom begins when you can recognize deception for what it is and stop going along with the lie. When you say "no more," you are drawing a line in the sand that says, "Devil, you aren't going to keep me from God with your lies."

The devil would have you to believe that he is a great "liberator" and that by living outside of God's will, you are "free." That's grade-A deception! Freedom is knowing that God is good to such a degree that you believe His Word and obey Him simply because you know it's always going to be in your best interest.

Freedom is knowing God and obeying His Word so that life is more of a joy than a chore. Sure, problems come to Christians and non-Christians alike, but with God, you've got some ammo on how to defeat the devil and reverse bad circumstances! Freedom is using

His Word so that you can find your way around the dirt of this world and live a peaceful, productive and healthy life – and know that you're going to Heaven when you die.

Freedom is *not* merely doing whatever your flesh tells you is good for the day. Look, if I did everything that felt good to me at the time, I'd be five hundred pounds and have a mind full of mush. I'd eat chicken legs and chocolate cake all day. They'd need a Mack truck to haul my big body to the grave!

Never Occupy a Place Where the Devil Should Be

I decided years ago that living for God was better and that there is nothing in Hell that I want! I chose to reject the devil and receive Jesus Christ as my Savior, because my soul needed saving. I didn't want to live without God and without hope. I didn't want to follow that fool devil down the dark path anymore because I didn't want to wind up living in his hellhole.

I've decided that I'm never going to occupy a place where the devil should be. Forget that! I'm not going to live where the worm never dies. Not me, son, I'm not going to end up where there is hot torment and bitter demons. I took care of my soul when I watched a Christian program on TV and then chose to turn my life over to God. I asked Jesus to come into my life in a bathroom in Boston, Massachusetts, in 1974. Now, every time I go to the "throne" I get happy!

Today, my life is dedicated to following Jesus Christ – and let me tell you something, it's a good life. And that's why I wrote this book. I want you to live a good life too, one that is better than you ever imagined it could be.

Jesus gave us all the answers we will ever need in this life – answers that lead to our salvation, healing, deliverance, prosperity, joy and victory. He paid for all those answers when He went to the cross. Jesus completely defeated the devil in every area and gave that power to you as a believer, when you accepted Him as Lord and Savior. Now, why did He do that? Because He knew that the devil was intent on ransacking your life!

In John 10:10-11, Jesus called the devil a thief who only comes, *"to steal, and to kill, and to destroy..."* but He made sure to tell us that He could save us when He said, *"I am come that they might have life, and that they might have it more abundantly. I am the good shepherd: the good shepherd giveth his life for the sheep."*

The devil may try to steal, kill and destroy your life, but that doesn't mean that it's inevitable that he's going to be successful. In Isaiah 54:17, the Word promises that, *"No weapon that is formed against thee shall prosper; and every tongue that shall rise against thee in judgment thou shalt condemn. This is the heritage of the servants of the LORD, and their righteousness is of Me, saith the LORD."*

You Have More Power Than You Think

You have a heritage of faith, and while the devil may formulate ways to harm you, the Bible says that his weapons won't prosper. But, you've got to have faith in God and know how to spot deception, temptation and use the Word to combat the devil. The simplest way to stop the devil in his tracks is to use the name of Jesus. Recognize the power that His name represents and remind yourself that Jesus gave *that* power to you! That ought to make you shout!

Yes, the devil will try to stop you and he'll use many different ways to try and get you to turn your back on God or simply lose out on the best that God has planned for your life. In this book, my aim is to show you many of the various ways the devil comes to stop the plan that God has for your life so that you can spot his lies and tell him where to go – Hell!

The devil is stupid – sneaky, but stupid. The boy hasn't figured out that he's the biggest loser that ever existed. He's fighting like he thinks he's going to win. Yet, the idiot knows that Jesus defeated him.

The devil *saw* Jesus nailed to the cross. He *saw* Jesus resurrected and ascending into Heaven with his own eyes. Can you believe that? The devil was there. He saw it all and yet, he still refuses to believe it. Now, that's just plain dumb. The Bible says he has been judged and will be cast out of this world. (See John 12:31, 16:11; 1 Corinthians 2:8) His mind is filled with so much rebellion and rage that he just can't think straight! He's losing it, man!

The more you read the Word and focus on God's power, the more you'll understand that no matter how much the devil does and how hard he tries, he is still the loser and Jesus is victorious!

Sin Gained a Foothold, but Jesus Exposed the Devil's Work

It bothers me that people give the devil more credit than he's worth. Sure, he was once a big dog in Heaven, but now, he's just a little bitty fire ant that God is going to send sailing in the blazing lake one day soon. I can hardly wait. That idiot and all his demons are going to pay for all the killing, stealing and destroying that they've done throughout our human history.

The Bible tells us in Romans 6:23, *"For the wages of sin is death..."* That's what the devil's going to get and everyone who rejects God and chooses to follow Satan – and it's a death much worse than mere human passing. When we die, we just shed this earth suit and move on, but when God says "death," it means an eternity without Him. As believers, we don't even have to consider the second death in Hell. Why? Because the rest of the verse tells us, *"...but the gift of God is eternal life through Jesus Christ our Lord."*

We just better thank God that He cared enough to send us "the gift" of eternal life through Jesus Christ! Without Jesus as our Savior, we would be without mercy and without hope, and that's a bad place to be. Jesus paid the price, buddy. He not only decided to give up His Heavenly privileges and die on the cross as a ransom for the sins of the world, but He also decided to *live* on this earth and avoid sinning. That's hard.

Think about it. When was the last time you met someone that never sinned? Even your religious Grandma had her day. Believe me, *everybody* has sinned and come short of the glory of God at one time or another.

We might say one sin is excusable and another is worthy of the death penalty, but in God's eyes, no matter how "small" the sin seems to be, it is something that has to be washed away in order to approach Him. The price for sin had to be paid for because nobody can make it through the pearly gates with sin hanging onto their soul.

We are all connected. God created us in His image and we are all His human family. The Bible tells us that all of humanity fell when Adam made a choice to rebel against God. Sin gained a foothold on the earth and everything changed because of it. That's why Jesus had to come. While it may seem wrong to think that you inherited the propensity to sin, it is just the bottom line truth. Sin lives in the heart of man.

Jesus is often called the second Adam because He made things right. Before Jesus came, we didn't know what was going on. Everybody who believed in God just assumed that everything good came from God and everything bad came from God. There was no real concept of the devil. When Jesus came over two thousand years ago, suddenly, mankind got the newsflash – there is a lying, stealing, killing and destroying devil out there! He's trying to wreak havoc on mankind just out of spite.

Demons, Imps and Other Idiots

In the New Testament, demons are talked about a lot more. They're recognized and often called things like unclean spirits, wicked spirits, evil spirits, deceiving spirits, demons and spirits of divination. Now, don't let the terminology whip your head around. Demons are losers. They may give themselves rank and power, but Jesus stripped them of all power over you at the cross.

An imp, a demon or whatever they want to call themselves and pretend to be, are all rejected by God. They've chosen their path, and they're without repentance. They are bent on killing, stealing and destroying as much as they can before they are sentenced to Hell without parole.

Today, people see movies about demons and they may joke about the devil, but the truth is that Lucifer and all his demons exist. We don't conjure these things up in our imaginations just to give us a thrill. They're based upon biblical truth and people throughout history have recognized evil as a reality. Evil is not just a "concept" or a "point of view." It's a reality of living in this world.

If you're interested, you can study the Bible to see the various types of demons, but Ephesians 6:12 gives you a clue when it says, *"For we wrestle not against flesh and blood, but against principalities, against powers, against the rulers of the darkness of this world, against spiritual wickedness in high places."*

I like it that this scripture warns us not to judge people as the culprit of wickedness in this earth. We are all just flesh and blood and I honestly believe that without a spirit deceiving or influencing them, most people would just turn to God without question.

This verse reminds us that there is more going on than meets the eye when it lists different terms to expose the demonic in this life – principalities, powers, rulers of the darkness in this world and spiritual wickedness that resides in high places. The Bible doesn't skirt the issue. There is a war going on in the spirit realm, whether people choose to recognize it or not.

But, you know, it doesn't really matter what kind of demon, imp or other idiot you encounter in this life because they are all restricted and defeated. *"Nay, in all these things we are more than conquerors through Him that loved us"* (Romans 8:37). Jesus has made you more than a conqueror over the devil, all his idiot cohorts and all his wicked works in this world. You've got everything you need in Jesus.

Realize Who is Backing You

You are so much further advanced than the devil and all his cohorts. You might not think you are, but you are. You've just got to realize Who is backing you – God Almighty. Fallen angels may be portrayed as more powerful than men and women of God in film and books, but that's just fantasy. One word can stop a demon in his tracks – Jesus. The Bible tells us, *"That at the name of Jesus every knee should bow, of things in heaven, and things in earth, and things under the earth; And that every tongue should confess that Jesus Christ is Lord, to the glory of God the Father"* (Phil. 2:10-11).

If the name of Jesus is used by a person who has faith, watch out! Every demon from Hell has to stand down! The Bible also tells us that after Jesus went to the cross for our sins, He earned the rightful position of top dog.

Ephesians 1:21-23 says Jesus was placed, *"**Far above** all principality, and power, and might, and dominion, and **every name that is named**, not only in this world, but also in that which is to come: And hath put all things **under his feet**, and gave Him to be **the head** over all things to the church, Which is **His body**, the fullness of Him that filleth all in all."*

If you meditate on that scripture, you are going to get a revelation of just how powerful Jesus is, and if you have accepted His redemption, how powerful He has made *you*.

Everything is under Jesus' feet – everything – including devils, demons, imps and everything they do. *"...For this purpose the Son of God was manifested, that he might destroy the works of the devil"* (1 John 3:8). Man, that makes me want to shout! I think I'm going to buy this book myself!

Satan's Greatest Tool – Deception

You see, the devil doesn't have any new tricks. The boy has an old repertoire and he's using the same old tactics on you that he's been using on mankind for thousands of years. What is his greatest tool? Deception!

The greatest tool the devil uses to defeat people in this life is not sickness, disease, poverty, discouragement, discontentment or disappointment. It's *deception*.

The devil lies! The Bible says, *"...he was a murderer from the beginning, and abode not in the truth, because there is no truth in him. When he speaketh a lie, he speaketh of his own: for he is a liar, and the father of it"* (John 8:44).

Everything he says is either an outright lie or a twisted truth. The devil will use his deceptive tactics like a tool to uproot your life and to steer you off course – to steal the good future that God has in store for you. If he can deceive your mind, then all those things I mentioned like discontent, discouragement and disappointment can work their way into your life. Those kinds of things can open the door to temptation, and if you aren't careful, you'll end up doing things you never thought you'd do.

I believe that **deception is the gateway to sin**. The devil doesn't try to tempt you before he first tries to deceive you. But, I believe that you can't be blindsided by his tactics if you, first, know what they are and, second, develop the character to use the Word. This is where having a relationship with Jesus comes in.

When you have God in your life, His spirit is living within you, and, if you tap into Him, He will help you to start developing "spiritualized common sense." Through the truths of His Word and His still, small voice speaking to your heart, God will open your eyes wide. Suddenly, you'll start to really *recognize* the devil's deceptive tactics in your life. That will give you the confidence to use the Word on the idiot and send him running for cover!

Demons Use Human Nature to Their Advantage

The devil isn't powerful, he's just deceitful. Because he and his cohorts have existed a lot longer than you, before the creation of this world in fact, they understand basic human nature and they will use that knowledge to their advantage.

What can you do about that? First, you stop giving them credit and then, you start concentrating on building up your own godly character. **If you don't strengthen what you have inside, you're not going to be able to fight off anything hitting you from outside**. It's time to take care of *you* so that you can use the Word with authority and put the devil in his place – under your blood-bought feet.

When you become strong inside, you'll start seeing the devil and all his devices for what they really are – deceiving attempts to hurt you and lure you away from God. You don't want to be away from God. Who wants Hell anyway? Remember that God is going to have to kick him in because he doesn't want Hell either! (See Revelations 19:20)

Character, Choice and New Habits

Living for God is about choice. It's about developing new habits. You can change anything you want to. It's not impossible to do, but it does take the guts to make a decision and the tenacity to stick to your commitment. This is the kind of life that starts when you wake up in the morning and decide to talk to God – to put Him first and do things His way.

If you have weak areas, and we all do, you're going to find that you can't resist the devil's deceptive tactics on your own – you really do need help and divine help is the best help there is. Character begins to develop when you say, "I'm not going to do things my way, God. I'm going to follow your way."

It's your relationship with God that not only saves you from Hell but saves you from yourself. It's your relationship with God that gives you the inner character you need to say "no" when the devil tries to deceive you and tempt you.

Right now, you've got all the power and authority you need to resist temptation. It's just time to start stoking your inner fire for God and start using your authority. With God, every weakness that you've had in the past can one day become your strength.

You may not know how God is going to do it, but if you stay on track with Him and just keep working on your character in the weak areas, you're going to one day be stronger than you ever thought you could be.

Sin

will take you further than **YOU** want to go...

The lure of green grass

The reality of sin

Chapter 3

The Greener the Grass, the Greater the Deception

Have you ever tried sleeping in a hotel room with no air-conditioning when it's as hot as Hell outside? I'll never forget when I first started preaching and a pastor put me in a hotel with no air-conditioning. It was Africa hot outside and I was sweating bullets. After a while, I said, "Lord, have you sweated enough? Can we get out of here?" Man, the words had hardly come from my lips when I heard a knock at the door.

"Bro. Jesse?" the person said, "I just felt impressed of the Lord to tell you that I have a beautiful pool house, if you want to stay there. You'll have privacy and everything. You can do what you want, but, would you like to stay there?"

I said, "I don't even need to pray about that. That's God!" I got out of the sweatbox and God blessed me with a cool place to be as I prepared for the rest of the revival services. You see, I figured out a long time ago that, wherever I go, God goes. If I'm sweating in a stinking, hot hotel room, He's with me! There is no place that I can go that I am alone.

But, sometimes, what *looks* good and *sounds* good isn't God's plan. That's why, when it comes to making major decisions in your life, you can't just look at the outside. You've got to consult with

God and recognize His hand on your life. He can steer you away from situations that seem good on the surface but are designed by the devil to steal away God's best plan for your life.

Now, this isn't easy! Sometimes an opportunity pops up that looks perfect in every way, and yet, you will know in your heart that it's not right. Why? The greener the grass, the greater the deception.

I've had many people tell me that I've "made it" in the ministry. They see me on television or they read a book of mine and say, "Man, you're doing good!" God has blessed me, but it's only because I've decided that I am going to stick with His plan – instead of my plan. I like green grass as much as the next guy, but there have been many times that God has told me "no" and I've listened.

There was a time when I wanted to move to Dallas so bad that I could spit. I hated Louisiana for years, but God told me to stay and I did. When friends of mine decided to "take a church" and settle into the role of a pastor, it looked like green grass to me too. I'm human and I like to sleep in my own bed too. I haven't always wanted to stay on the road, traveling with the Gospel, but God told me to stick with my calling – and I'm an evangelist. Since 1978, I've been evangelizing and God has never changed my calling.

Sure, there have been times I've wanted to give up, maybe take a "greener" path. Take the time a large church in Texas called me. I don't know how they got a tape of me preaching, but when they called to ask me to join their preaching staff, the timing was just perfect.

Living By the Faith of Jesus

You see, I'd been traveling extensively and I was struggling financially. God was taking care of me, but just barely. These were in the "sowing" years – the years that I preached for two dollars a week or a Dr. Pepper, when "eating out" meant a trip to McDonald's for a small cheeseburger. Man, if I had five dollars to spring on a Quarter Pounder with cheese, I felt like I was spending the big bucks! So, when I got the call, it was like seeing green in the middle of the desert.

The man who called me was very polite. He said, "Rev. Duplantis, we have heard some of your tapes and we would like you to be a part of this staff." I was shocked.

"Yeah," he went on, "We've got about six thousand people here and I really believe you could really help our Sunday night meetings."

I said to myself, *You better know I can, son! Praise God!*

He continued sharing about the church and then said, "We want you to come and preach every Sunday night. You can still go out and do all of your own meetings, but we need you here every Sunday night. If you'll do that, we will purchase you a home."

Now, at that time, I traveled so much, I felt like I was living out of the back of my Toyota! For me, home was a nine hundred square foot roach hole in South Louisiana where I could sit on the john and put my hands in the lavatory at the same time. Of course, I only spent two or three nights a week in that mini-house, but the rest was on the road. So, to hear the words "church staff" and "home" in the same sentence sounded like a miracle of God.

"We'll pay you fifteen hundred dollars a night," the man said. I didn't think I'd heard correctly so I said, "How much?"

He said, "We want you to preach 35 to 50 minutes every Sunday night and we'll pay you fifteen hundred dollars a Sunday night. We will buy you a home and we will give you an office."

"This is God," I said to myself, "This is God. Yes, this is God!" Well, I spoke with the man a bit more and told him that I'd pray about it and get back with him soon. When I hung up, I was flying high. I couldn't stop saying, "This is God! This is God! This is God!" In my mind, surely, this was God's best, His perfect will for my life. The problem was that He wasn't agreeing with me.

I prayed and prayed, "Come on, God. Say something, but say the right thing!" Today, I know that when God doesn't want me to do something, He just doesn't say a word. He puts the silent treatment on me! He wants me to search my heart.

"Would you like to speak a word to me, Lord? This is nice, this will help us!" I prayed, and then when I realized what was going on. I said, "Okay, what's the problem? We got a problem here?!" Then, He spoke up. "Yeah, we have a problem. You should not be there."

"But, why? Why?" I asked.

"That's neither here nor there. I didn't call you there," God said.

"They did!" I said. Man, I was trying to pitch my tent toward the Dallas/Fort Worth area. I even told Cathy about it, but she didn't see the color of the green grass the way I did.

"You know, that is a wonderful offer, but it isn't right," she said. I was aggravated and so I snapped, "God made you second! He made me first. Listen woman!" Then, I went on to tell her all the good points of the offer again and again. She didn't seem too fazed, and I just couldn't understand it.

Do you ever wonder why men just don't understand women? It's because we were asleep when God created them. We woke up and there she was – beautiful but with a look that said, "I'm boss." Things haven't changed much. (It's just a joke!)

I said, "God? Why?"

"That's not for you," He said.

"Are you sure?"

He said, "Trust me."

Trusting the Lord in "Brown Grass" Times

Well, I gave in and decided to obey God. Even though I really wanted the position, I called the church back and graciously declined their offer. They were so kind. They told me to call them if I changed my mind and left the position open to me, even after their senior pastor passed away not long after.

I was mad at God for about six months. Every time I slept in another bad hotel or was treated to a "forced fast" by a pastor who stole the offering, I remembered that church. Why? Green grass! They were a wonderful church and there wasn't anything wrong with them, but they just weren't in God's plan for my life. He didn't want me to be a pastor living in Texas. He called me to be an evangelist based out of Louisiana.

What would have happened if I would have taken the position? I would have been out of God's will for my life, and that is not a fun place to be. Sure, I would have been blessed in some ways, but I would be forfeiting God's best and I would have been more vulnerable to attack from the devil.

You see, when you knowingly disobey God's instruction, you step out of His will and you are saying, "I want what I want more than I want what God wants for me. I know best." You don't know best. Green grass is deceptive. I've seen many people living hellish lives simply because they gave in to the temptation to follow every green patch of grass that popped up before them in life. They were led around by their flesh instead of by what the Spirit of God was saying, and that makes for a hellish life.

Well, for six months, the Lord dealt with my attitude concerning that church and I repented for being angry at Him. But, the situation taught me a very valuable lesson about trusting God and recognizing that the greener the grass, the greater the deception.

Since then, I've decided that no matter how good something looks, if it isn't from God, it's not for me. The best path is the one that God chooses for me to take, and if I just follow His instruction, using the Word and the still, small voice, He will never steer me wrong. My job is to trust in the Lord, to stick it out when I feel like quitting and finish my course with joy.

Today, the blessings of God follow me. Don't get mad at me if I'm blessed! I've obeyed, I've trusted and I've put my faith out there for miracles knowing that God is going to do what He said if I stick with Him through the "brown grass" times.

Psalm 37:3-4 says that blessings are bound to happen to those who trust God: *"Trust in the LORD, and do good; so shalt thou dwell in the land, and verily thou shalt be fed. Delight thyself also in the LORD; and He shall give thee the desires of thine heart."* I believe that God is giving me the desires of my heart today because I chose to go His way in the brown grass times.

Pick a Plot, Lot

Lot had a problem with the green grass and it turned his life into a living hell. When God told Abraham to leave his extended family, get out of town and go to a place He'd show him, Abraham did it...well, he did it 90% of the way. The Bible says that Abraham asked his nephew, Lot, to go along for the ride and this little bending of God's command ended up causing Abraham and Lot problems. You see, God's hand of blessing was on Abraham, but it wasn't on Lot. Why? He didn't belong there.

Well, Abe and Lot settled into their new land and God began to prosper Abraham. God had blessed Abraham for his obedience and God made him very rich in cattle, silver and gold. He was so blessed with livestock that things were getting crowded on the land. There just wasn't enough room on the land for everyone to live peacefully. It wasn't long before strife between Abraham and Lot's workers cropped up. *"And there was strife between the herdmen of Abram's cattle and the herdmen of Lot's cattle: and the Canaanite and the Perizzite dwelled then in the land"* (Genesis 13:7).

You can take it to the bank that when strife crops up, the devil is close by! Strife is one of the ways that he tries to ruin good relationships. Abraham didn't want there to be problems in the family, so he decided to make Lot an offer that he couldn't refuse.

And Abram said unto Lot, Let there be no strife, I
pray thee, between me and thee, and between my

herdmen and thy herdmen; for we be brethren.

Is not the whole land before thee? Separate thyself, I pray thee, from me: if thou will take the left hand, then I will go to the right; or if thou depart to the right hand, then I will go to the left.

Genesis 13:8-9

Abraham offered Lot half of all the land. He even went so far as to offer Lot any side he wanted. That's pretty generous. Why didn't Abraham worry about what side of land he was going to end up with? He was nonchalant about it because Abraham knew that God would be with him, no matter what kind of land he ended up with. Abraham trusted that God would take care of him.

The Green Grass Next Door to Sodom

Now, I want to point out what Lot does at this point. Verse ten says, *"And Lot lifted up his eyes and beheld all the plain of Jordan, that it was well watered every where, before the Lord destroyed Sodom and Gomorrah, even as the garden of the Lord, like the land of Egypt, as thou comest unto Zoar."* Notice that Lot looked around. He immediately used his senses, and didn't pray about it at all. He was looking at what he thought was green grass.

Then Lot chose him all the plain of Jordan; and Lot journeyed east: and they separated themselves the one from the other.

Abram dwelled in the land of Canaan, and Lot dwelled in the cities of the plain, and pitched his tent toward Sodom.

*But the men of Sodom were wicked and sinners before
the Lord exceedingly.*

Genesis 13:11-13

Why did Lot choose to pitch his tent toward Sodom? Green grass!
He looked over the place and thought everything looked good. He
figured that since Abraham had most of the money, he could maybe
make a lot of money where the green grass grew. But, Lot didn't
consider that the green grass backed up to a sinful place. He was
about to start living where temptation was just up the road.

Now, the next time the Bible talks about Lot, we find out that
Lot is living right smack in the middle of Sodom. Why? Because he
pitched his tent *toward* Sodom. He was on his way the moment he
decided to rely only on his senses. Remember, sin will take you
further than you want to go; keep you longer than you want to stay;
and charge you more than you want to pay.

Sodom was attractive to Lot. Why? It was a place were the five
senses ruled. The flesh is weak, and unless you do what Paul said,
it's easy to make bad choices. You have to "crucify" your flesh so
that you won't "fulfill the lust of the flesh." In other words, a
dead man can't do anything. If he sees something attractive, but
wrong, he just says, "Well, I'm a dead man" and he goes about his
business, doing what God told him to do. But notice this, the grass
near Sodom *looked* good.

There are a lot of things out there that will look good, but you
can take it to the bank, where the grass is too green, there is usually
deception. It's like a lady told me once at a church I was guest

speaking, "I'm leaving this church! Bless God, I don't like this church. I'm going over to that church cause that church is really flowing." I said, "Lady, let me tell you something. That looks like green grass to you but there are manure piles over there too. You just hadn't seen the place up close."

You see, temptations will always look beautiful and prosperous on the surface, but what the devil shows is always meant to deceive you – and to steal everything from you. When Lot pitched his tent toward Sodom, he had cattle, a family and some money.

By the time Sodom got through with Lot, he had nothing but his two daughters. Lot lost his wife, his herdsmen, cattle and just about everything else simply because he thought the green grass was where he should be. Although he tried to do right, Lot made the mistake of letting the evils of Sodom draw him nearer and nearer. The devil deceived him and stole from him.

God Can Turn Brown Grass Green

I've made up my mind to follow God instead of just my senses. If God calls me to a desert, all I have to do is pray over the place and He will irrigate it and make it green. It doesn't have to start out looking good; God can make it good in the end.

Once a man in South Louisiana asked me, "How can I prosper if I'm in an area of low economy?" The Lord spoke to my heart and said, "Tell him I put six million people on a desert and Exxon wasn't there." You see, South Louisiana prospers according to the oil industry, but God wanted me to let this man know that He was able to provide regardless of the local economy.

Sometimes we limit God, but He is a creator. He rained fifteen hundred tons of bread on the ground for the children of Israel. He gave them thousands of gallons of water to quench their thirst, as well as all of their animals' thirst. He wasn't worried about Sinai! He is God!

If I was hungry, walking along and God dropped a hunk of bread on me, I don't think I'd complain and say, "How about a jar of peanut butter?" But, that's kind of what the people did. They actually got so accustomed to the miracles that they started complaining. So, God threw them millions of quail! He can do anything. So, it doesn't make a difference what the situation looks like, He can make brown grass turn green if you'll stick with Him.

King Solomon was the richest man who ever lived, but there came a time in his life when he went searching for peace in material and fleshly things. He lost his focus and ended up miserable. The Bible quotes him listing possession upon possession, and, in the end, calling it all vanity. You see, it's vanity to chase after riches. I believe in prosperity and preach on it because it's in the Word, but the Bible tells us that we shouldn't chase anything but God. If we put our trust in Him and seek after His way of doing things, He will *reward* us with material things. If we use His system of sowing, we will reap. Trusting in God and doing things His way is how Abraham got blessed and kept his joy.

This life is full of choices. You can choose life or death. You can choose to walk with God or pitch your tent towards Sodom. Never forget that there are devils out there, and they fertilize the grass ahead of you. They will give you a view of beautiful and alluring scenery that you may think looks just perfect. It may be a relationship, a business venture, a new locale or a new church. Pray before you choose where you're going to pitch your tent, because under that green grass may be some carcinogenic chemicals!

God's best is for you. He wants you to be prosperous and eat the good of the land. But, it will take a while for you to get back to His best if you get sidetracked. So, always remember that God is with you. Whether you go left or right, He will prosper you and guide you, but He's going to need you to use more than just your five senses. That is going to be developed in your life by practice.

You have to practice using faith before it comes easily. You get up and go to church, even when you don't feel like it; you feed your spirit with scriptures that will build you up; you read books and listen to tapes; and you do what you have to do to get strong inside, and practice doing what you learn. The stronger you are inside, the easier it will be to handle the green grass outside.

Don't jump at the chance to run on the devil's green grass. Pray. Listen to God's voice. If you do, you'll learn how to spot the devil's deception a mile away. You'll learn how to put your flesh down and say "no" to those impulses to do only what looks and feels good. God is going to make you strong, even in the area where you are weak. Trust Him and remember, the greener the grass, the greater the deception.

Chapter 4

Don't Go Further Than You Want to Go

Years ago I was preaching in Shreveport, Louisiana, and after a powerful, Holy Ghost-punching service, I was headed back to my hotel room. I was staying at the Sheraton Piermont Hotel, and as I was in the lobby, a beautiful woman approached me.

"Would you like to have some company for the evening?" she asked me.

I just looked at her for a moment and then I said, "I'm a dead man."

"Oh," she said, "I'm sorry."

I said, "Honey, I've got a lot of company. I've got God the Father, God the Son, and God the Holy Ghost. I'm filled with the Spirit from the top of my head to the soles of my feet. I know Jesus!" That woman didn't wait for me to say another word. She took off running! Now, I didn't tell her to run, but she couldn't help it. She was compelled to get away from me!

Now, I could have said, "Hey, what's happening, mama!?" I knew the devil was trying to resurrect my flesh. He was saying, "Come on. Wake up, Jesse. Wake up, wake up, wake up..." but I'd decided to stay dead. Why? I've learned to recognize his tactics.

These things happen for a reason. The devil comes to steal, to kill and to destroy, and when he tempts my flesh, he's really trying to use deception to target the work of God. I've come to realize that when the devil tempts me, there is more at stake than just me and my wife; there are thousands and maybe millions of other people who need to hear about Jesus Christ through my ministry. If I mess around, I not only dishonor myself, my wife and my God, but I blow my witness to people that God intended for me to reach for Him.

That night, when I got to my hotel room, I called my wife and told her I'd been hit on. The woman didn't miss a beat. She flew to Shreveport the next day! I thought that was funny. Women are like cats, man, they mark their territory. It's a miracle of God that they don't spray their husbands down before leaving the house!

For the rest of the week, Cathy scanned the lobby every time we walked through it and asked me, "Is she anywhere around? Where is she?" I never did see the woman. For all I know, she ran to the next town!

What is Sin?

When most people hear the word "sin" they think of things like adultery. They think of things like murder and child pornography. Anything over-the-top bad is considered sin to most people. But, do you know the true meaning of sin? It is simply "missing the mark" – and you can do that on the highway today by just cussing out the guy who swerved in front of you!

"The mark" is God's bull's-eye. It's what you know in your heart to be right and what the Word says is right. It's the way God has asked you to live – not in the flesh, but in faith and in Christ. You hit the bull's-eye when you crucify your flesh and let Him live through you.

When you separate yourself and live independent from your Maker, you're heading straight for sin. You're on your own and pretty soon, it's not just going to affect your life but those around you.

Obey the "Tapping" of God

It may seem like an outdated idea today, but if you've fallen into that way of thinking – you are deceived. Sin is real. It will steal from you. I don't care who tells you that it's OK and that it won't hurt anything. If God said it, and you know in your heart it is true, don't push that inner "tap" away.

Sin is not just another name for human imperfection and mistakes. Sin is simple rebellion against the will of God.

You know when God is "tapping" you on the inside. You know when His voice is saying, "Don't do it, don't do that." If you choose to do it anyway, you're sinning, and I don't care if it's over a prostitute, a crack pipe or a huge piece of chocolate cake. You're going to have to repent because you've "missed the mark."

Don't Grade Sin

Christians may say that "sin is sin" but most don't believe that anymore than they believe the moon is made of cheese. It doesn't seem to matter what Christian denomination you belong to, everybody, whether they admit it or not, judges and grades sin.

We may not use the words "mortal sin" or "venial sin" but we think it! You can see it in the way we react to other people's sin and in the way that we talk about sin in general.

Think about it. Most people would jump all over a preacher for committing adultery, but if that same preacher happens to get angry at somebody in the church and runs them out of town, people let it go. They not only forgive it, they forget about it. But sexual sin is something they never forget!

They Broke One, Moses Broke Ten

Moses is considered pretty spiritual by most people, but even the "best" of spiritual people lose it from time to time. Everyone can get out of balance and everyone needs forgiveness.

When Moses came down the mountain with the Ten Commandments, he found all the people worshiping a golden image and he got as mad as a hornet. He took the Commandments, threw them on the ground and broke them! Why? He was mad at the people! He didn't think they deserved them! But, that wasn't his place to decide. It's funny that the people broke one commandment, but Moses broke ten!

Moses went slap crazy and got in the flesh. What did God do? He sent Moses back up the mountain to get another set. In other words, God forgave Him and restored His purpose.

You may sin, but if you repent and turn back to God, He will forgive you and restore your purpose. You may detour and take longer to get to your destiny, but you are never lost or hopeless if you stick with God.

Remember this when you see somebody else fall into sin. They may break one commandment and you may want to throw ten at them! You may get angry at them for what they've done and want to break something, but guess what? You aren't Moses and you aren't God. You may be more like one of those people dancing around the golden image and you've got no right to cast the first stone. Let God be God.

Everything Balances on Love

Avoiding sin gets a whole lot easier when you start recognizing Jesus, the Person, more than Christianity as a religion. It continues to get easier when you start recognizing and adhering to Jesus' two simple rules for living this life.

> *Jesus said unto him,* **Thou shalt love the Lord thy God with all thy heart,** *and with all thy soul, and with all thy mind.*
> *This is the first and great commandment.*
> *And the second is like unto it,* **Thou shalt love thy neighbour as thyself.**
> *On these two commandments hang all the law and the prophets.*
>
> Matthew 22:37-40

Everything is balanced on those two "love rules." Every Christian denomination we have today stemmed from Christ's teaching. Each denomination may focus on one area of the Word more than another – maybe grace, maybe faith, maybe love, but all of them came into existence because of Jesus Christ and His miraculous birth, life and teachings, crucifixion and resurrection. But, what stands at the center of it all is the golden rule.

After all, if you love God with all your heart, mind and soul, why would you hurt Him by destroying your body, polluting your mind or hurting other people?

If lust is your problem, consider the fact that the very person you are lusting after is made in God's image. God loves that person and wants them to be whole, healthy and understand their value as more than a fleshly object – as a person who Jesus died for on the cross.

If you love the Lord with all your heart, you'll draw close to Him. If you love Him with all your mind, you'll care about what He cares about. You'll start focusing on thinking His way. If you love Him with all your soul, your will and emotions will begin to reflect it. God will rub off on you and you will start to not only see your own value, but see the value of others. People are worth more than the whole world to God! They shouldn't be used, abused, hurt, battered, stolen from or made to feel guilt and shame. They are human beings, made in the image of God.

What You're Really Searching for Can Only Come from God

You can spend your life looking for people who will stroke your ego or make you feel good by telling you nice words. You can spend your life looking for people and things that make you feel desirable. Guess what? You don't want those things and you don't even want those people. What you want is the feeling of being desired, loved, cherished, respected, admired, etc. What person on earth can fill that void? Nobody can do it. It's too big of a job.

If you've got self-esteem problems and look to others to fill you up with compliments, start focusing on loving God with all your heart, mind and soul. He'll show you how to love yourself so that you can stop making other people and what they think about you a priority.

Only God can give you what you really want. Only God, and maybe your mama, can make you feel wanted and loved unconditionally! People are human and they are going to fail. They're going to treat you wrong. They can't fill a place in your heart where God is supposed to be. What they say and do for you won't have a lasting effect in your mind or your heart because they can't provide the all-consuming love of God.

When you focus on giving love to God, you'll be amazed at how much you feel His love flooding your mind, your heart and your soul. It will change your perspective on how to live and treat other people. You'll get so much of His love in you that you'll start wanting to give it to somebody else. You'll become generous, even if you've been stingy your entire life!

How do you love others as you love yourself? By crucifying your flesh and letting Jesus live through you. You can't give that kind of love to others on your own, but with Jesus living through you, you can do it.

How can you steal from somebody else if you love them as you love yourself? How can you hurt someone who is close to you if you love them as you love yourself? You can't! The moral ethic becomes a by-product of your faith in the Person, Jesus Christ. You see, Jesus knew that if we could get our heart right, the rest would follow.

Study the Word with the Right Heart

Have you ever heard someone use the Word as an excuse to miss the mark? 2 Timothy 2:15 says, *"Study to show thyself approved unto God, a workman that needeth not to be ashamed, rightly dividing the word of truth."* If your heart is right, when you study the Word, you're going to be able to *rightly* divide the Word of truth. If you don't have the right **heart** because you haven't considered Jesus' two "love rules" and you don't **study the Word**, it's possible that you could *wrongly* divide the truth.

Anybody using the Bible as an excuse to do whatever their flesh tells them isn't rightly dividing the truth. They don't have the right heart and they may not have studied at all! They may not even care about God and just want to use scripture to manipulate others.

The scripture was given to us to promote God's glory in the earth and teach us how to live this life well so that we can be healthy, whole, joyful, peaceful, loving, successful, merciful, etc.

If you search the Word, you'll see that Jesus never once used scripture to manipulate anyone or as an excuse to miss the mark. He used it primarily to teach others, but He also used the Word to personally resist the devil's temptation to sin.

Nobody Has the Right to Judge

Many people have different ideas about what "missing the mark" is all about. I find that people are just plain slaphappy about using their own specific doctrines to judge others.

When I was a rock musician, shooting drugs and drinking myself to an early death, where were the church people? In my generation, they were sitting in church picking on each other like monkeys.

I was dying and going to Hell, and they were pointing fingers at one another and judging each other for every stinking little flaw, picking on each other like monkeys in a zoo. They were pointing fingers: "Look at that man, my God, smoking them cigarettes! Don't he know he's going to Hell?" And they were sitting there with a fifty-pound belly hanging over their belt!

The women would eyeball anyone with a drop of lipstick on and say, "That woman looks like a Jezebel!" Nobody in the church ever saw Jezebel. There wasn't anybody that old! It used to make me angry as a teenager when I'd hear someone tell the congregation to live right from the pulpit, but then they'd run off with the piano player the next week. That's the kind of stuff that was happening while I was rejecting Jesus and going to Hell.

The world was playing great music, and the church was stuck in "Amazing Grace." Great song, but I was listening to Led Zeppelin and Grand Funk. My point is that if we're Christians, we don't have to act just like the world but we have to keep up in life and not get stuck in our ways so much that we can't identify with others anymore. It's not our right to judge another generation.

Too many Christians want to crucify other Christians instead of crucifying their own flesh. I can't stand it when I hear people from one denomination tell those in another denomination, "Well, if you don't believe exactly our way, then you're going to Hell!" I heard that all my life. Listen, nobody has the right or ability to execute judgment on a person's soul but God – nobody!

As a Christian, God wants you to be more adept in checking your own heart instead of looking for other people's sin. Jesus was point-blank blunt in telling us to mind our own business first.

> And why beholdest thou the mote that is in thy brother's eye, but considerest not the beam that is in thine own eye?
> Or how wilt thou say to thy brother, Let me pull out the mote out of thine eye; and, behold, a beam is in thine own eye?
> Thou hypocrite, first cast out the beam out of thine own eye; and then shalt thou see clearly to cast out the mote out of thy brother's eye.
>
> Matthew 7:3-5

The more you focus on somebody else's problem or sin, the less you focus on your own – and that's just a recipe for trouble! Let me tell you something. It's easy to get deceived into thinking that your way is the best way, but God's way is the only good way. He is the only judge, but there are a lot of people trying to steal His job!

So, what should you do? Concentrate on just sharing Jesus' teachings with the right heart – based first on the two main commandments, Jesus' "love rules." Then, study His teachings so that when you share the truth, you're sharing it right! If you let God do His job, you'll not only be a whole lot happier, but you'll have a lot more peace too.

People are much harder on other people than God ever is. People will give you all the "do's" and the "don'ts," but God is first and foremost interested in your heart. He wants you to focus on Him, because He is focused on you.

Who do you love? What are you doing? What is your motivation? Are you looking to Jesus as the author and finisher of your faith, or are you so in tune with what the world is doing that you just follow every impulse as they come?

The Bible tells you that while people look on the outside appearances, God looks on the heart. He is interested in saving mankind, not only from Hell, but also from a hellish lifetime of "missing the mark."

Have Compassion, Not Sympathy

Compassion is a word that we've come to think of as "sympathy," but that's not what Jesus had for people who were hurting or even living in sin. Sympathy means you just feel sorry for somebody, but compassion means you care for them enough to be motivated to *do* something for them.

Jesus saw people who missed the mark as simply "sheep without a Shepherd," and He sought to help them find the way to God – through sincerity, faith and doing right. The only time He really got angry with people in the Bible was when they used religion to cover up their own impure motives and hypocrisy. The rest of the time, Jesus continued pointing people to His Father.

Jesus' ministry was dedicated to preaching and doing good. Notice that Jesus didn't just *talk* about healing, He healed people. He didn't just talk about delivering people, He delivered them from oppression. He didn't just talk about the Word of God, He lived it too. He was adamant about teaching people the truth so that they could turn to God and *stop* "missing the mark" all the time.

This is what compassion does. It's what God has for you every time you mess up and miss the mark. He is always looking for ways to bring you back to exactly where you once were with Him. He's releasing the blood of Jesus to wash the sin away. He's tapping your heart saying, "Come on. Recognize what the devil is doing. You're stronger than he will ever be."

Don't Go Further Than You Want to Go

There are all sorts of religions in the world that tell you that you must *do* something to earn redemption. Christianity is the only world religion in which you don't have to *earn* righteousness. You just have to accept that Jesus Christ is God's Son and that He agreed to take all your blame. He paid the highest price when He gave His life for humanity.

One of the things I love about Jesus Christ is that, during His earthly ministry, He preferred to be called the Son of Man...even though He was the Son of God and made no denial of it. He just loved people so much! He was honored to give His life for us. I love that!

Jesus is also the only spiritual leader who died *and* rose again with over five hundred witnesses seeing Him after His death. Nobody else resurrected! The birth, life, death and resurrection of Jesus fulfilled prophecies from the Old Testament too.

If you really study Jesus, you'll find that no man has ever spoken like Him or lived like Him. He revolutionized the world in only three short years of ministry. That's because He wasn't just a prophet, He was divine. Yet, the Bible says He emptied Himself of all privilege in order to give Himself as a sacrifice for mankind – to give us the opportunity to be righteous by merely recognizing His act and asking God to help us.

All we've got to do is simply believe and accept Jesus Christ. It's simple, but it's the only thing that the Bible says God accepts. Once we accept Jesus, then God sees us through the veil of His sacrifice. What Jesus did flows onto us…and that's what makes us righteous in God's eyes.

To be saved and have your sins washed away, all you have to do is believe it in your heart and confess it with your mouth that Jesus is Lord. If you fall into missing the mark after that, and you will do that sometimes because you're not perfect, all you have to do is repent and the Bible says that the sin will be washed away, never to be remembered against you anymore. It's that simple.

People try to make salvation hard because they believe it must be earned. It's a gift. They try to make repentance hard because they believe that the blood couldn't possibly wash away sin that quickly. They're wrong. The blood is powerful and can wash any sin clean – no matter when it was committed.

You see, God is merciful and the moment you say, "I repent. Lord, please forgive me." God is right there with the redeeming blood of Jesus. He washes it away and in the same moment, encourages you to "Go and sin no more" – to start living clean again.

Sin
will keep
YOU *longer*
than you want to stay...

Exercise your power

Live clean in a dirty world

CHAPTER 5

You Can Live Clean in a Dirty World

This is one dirty world. Until you get to Heaven, you're going to have to deal with finding ways around the dirt. In this world, people are going to sin and do things you never thought they would do. They're going to kill each other, steal from each other and pollute their minds and bodies. They're going to live like animals and treat each other like dogs. It's going to continue even after they die.

After the great white throne judgment, the Bible says that some people will be cast into *outer* darkness where there is gnashing of teeth. I don't think that sounds good. I'd never want anyone gnashing around me! I'm glad I'm not going to Hell!

So, evil is here to stay, but just because evil is all around you doesn't mean you have to act accordingly. You can live clean, even in a very evil and dirty world. I tell people that I've had many opportunities to fail – I just didn't take any. That's not arrogance; that's confidence in the power of God. I've decided to live the way Jesus said I could live – holy. How do I do that? By living in a crucified body.

I've made up my mind that the God in me is stronger than the temptation to fall, and if I'll just choose wisely when temptation comes, I'll be alright. God has promised me that I'll always have a way of escape from temptation. I've promised Him that I will do my best to always take the escape route!

Don't Quarantine Yourself!
Strengthen Yourself!

People think that when they choose God's ways that they have to quarantine themselves from the rest of society. I used to tell my daughter, "You don't have to be a monk. Just love God." Let me tell you something, Jesus didn't quarantine Himself away from all sin, sickness and evil men. There were times that He got alone to pray, fast and just have quiet time with God, but He spent His life among people. He went to parties and He ate dinner with sinners. And, Jesus wasn't just a teacher of the Word; He was an example to the world.

I don't believe in sheltering yourself from all sin. I believe in developing a strong relationship with God so that, when you're confronted with sin, you choose to resist it and follow God instead. If you just focus on what you're *not* going to be around, you're not developing your own spiritual strength. God's purity has to get inside of you and push out the pollution of the world. You have to decide that, with Him, you are strong.

When God delivered me from alcoholism, people told me that I should never put myself in the position of having another drink. That may have sounded good to them, but it was plain foolish to me. Just about every restaurant serves scotch, and I needed to eat out sometimes. I still went to parties. I didn't die to life when I got saved; I just died to the sin. So, I threw their advice out the window and chose to focus on what God said in His Word.

Jesus never said, "Go and never enter a place where they serve booze again." He said, "Go and sin no more." The sin was the issue, so the sin nature is what had to be addressed. After all, that's what crucifying the flesh is all about – denying the sin nature in favor of God's nature.

To me, it wouldn't have mattered if somebody was sitting right next to me slugging down my favorite liquor – God saved me from that life and I didn't want it anymore. If an inkling of an urge came over me to drink, I rejected it fiercely in my own mind and with my mouth. I talked to the devil, "I rebuke you, devil!" I figured that God had forgiven me too much for me to slide back to those old ways. That was my mindset then, and it's still my mindset today.

Jesus Won't Condemn You

Some people like to tell me that it's impossible to not sin. They think it's something you have to do everyday. That is just a lie from the pit of Hell!

Jesus wouldn't have told the woman who was being stoned for her sin to *"go and sin no more"* unless it was possible for her to indeed go and sin no more. That woman was caught in the very act of adultery, which, in that time and place, was punishable by stoning. Obviously, Jesus didn't agree with the law.

When her accusers attacked her, she ran to Jesus for help and He spoke up on her behalf by challenging the crowd with, *"...he that is without sin among you, let him first cast a stone at her"* (John 8:7). When no one condemned her to death, Jesus said, *"Neither do I condemn thee: go, and sin no more"* (John 8:11). Jesus wasn't looking for an opportunity to hurt the woman but to save the woman.

He wants to do the same for you. If you mess up and run to Him for help and forgiveness, He will not condemn you. He will save you from paying the price of sin by releasing His blood on your behalf.

Don't be nervous about running to Jesus with your problem. When you confess your sin, it won't be the first time He has heard about it. You can't pull a fast one over on the Lord! He sees everything! But, it is good for you to be honest before Him and repent. He will always be faithful and just to forgive you.

Remember, like Romans 3:23 says, you may have *"...sinned, and come short of the glory of God"* but you don't have to sin every day. With the Lord's help, you can obey Jesus' words to *"Go and sin no more"* and start living clean again.

The Root Issue – Your Heart

Religious people will always try and hound you with the "don'ts." They don't focus on the root issue, which is the heart. Religious people will have you believe that you should quarantine yourself from society once you get saved. They did it to Jesus.

> *But their scribes and Pharisees murmured against his disciples, saying, Why do ye eat and drink with publicans and sinners?*
>
> *And Jesus answering said unto them, They that are whole need not a physician; but they that are sick.*
>
> *I came not to call the righteous, but sinners to repentance.*
>
> Luke 5:30-32

Jesus knew that weak people needed strength. He knew that the sick needed a doctor, and He was there to be a blessing among the sick. God told us in His Word to be a light in a dark place. He knows you're going to be surrounded by darkness and He wants you to be an example. *"Let your light so shine before men, that they may see your good works, and glorify your Father which is in Heaven"* (Matt. 5:16).

If you just allow yourself to keep on falling into sin, what kind of example are you setting for others who don't know about Christ? Sure, you'll be forgiven and God will restore you, but it's a whole lot better to just live right in the first place. It's less frustrating for yourself and God's grace.

It may not seem easier when temptation is raging, but it will be easier when you don't have to deal with the repercussions of sin. Don't let the devil lie to you and tell you that you can't resist temptation. Of course, you can. You aren't weak. With God, you are strong. Make your decision to stay clean – to resist the devil and take God's escape route when it makes itself known.

"Kill 'Em All, Jesus! Especially My Mother-in-law!"

One time I was mad at a bunch of Christians because they served *Chris* and I served *Christ*. They had done me wrong and I wanted vengeance. I said, "Lord?" He didn't even let me finish talking. He said, "Pray for them." I said, "Kill 'em all, Jesus!" I had to repent!

Another time, I was mad at my mother-in-law...for twelve years. I didn't like that woman and she didn't like me. In fact, I told the Lord, "If she goes to Heaven, it will ruin it for me!" I was as serious as I could be. Now, she wasn't born again, but I was. That's the sad part. I didn't really want her to get saved. I could have cared less if she knew Jesus or not. I wanted God to kill her and take her out of my life.

From the day I met her until the day God dealt with my heart, I hated my mother-in-law's guts. The day I met her, she looked me up and down and flat out told me, "I don't like you." I looked at that old bat and retorted, "Well, I ain't much on you either." She turned her nose up at me and that was it.

The problem was that we had a common denominator – her daughter. Now, I can't even tell you about the battles that went on between my mother-in-law and me. The woman had a gift for sarcasm that rivaled none, and back then, I could get madder than a hornet at the drop of a hat, so we didn't exactly match up, personality-wise. But I will say this, one of the hardest things I've ever done is forgive that woman!

When God told me to "love her," I thought He was nuts. "Love her Yourself," I said. The Lord said, "Pray for her." I wanted to tell Him that I was fine with her going to Hell, but He started convicting my heart. There I was, a Christian, and I couldn't even be in the same room with my mother-in-law.

It all started to change when I decided to let go of my way and start doing things God's way. I let the purity of the Gospel go as far as the pollution of my anger. I began to pray for her and that tension between us began to break. Now, I'm not saying we started loving each other the minute I started praying, but things definitely got easier. I started going out of my way to be civil, and then nice and that hatred started just melting away. It wasn't really very long before we actually started getting along – and laughing about how mean we used to be.

Today, my mother-in-law knows the Lord, and, amazingly, she loves me! If you say something bad about me, that woman will get in your face. She protects me and stands up for me. I do the same for her. I love her, and that's a miracle, son!

You know, sometimes a person just rubs you the wrong way. Certain personalities don't click – they cluck! But, when you're a believer, you have a way around that. You can break the spirit that is motivating you to hate. You can let God's Spirit motivate you to love, even those you are tempted to slap!

Mowing the Lawn and Listening to the Devil

Be honest. Haven't you ever wanted God to use a little vengeance? Maybe you got mad at somebody at work, in the church…in your own house.

One time, I was really mad at Cathy and the devil was talking to me about it. I was cutting my grass in the backyard. This was years ago. I don't cut my grass anymore. I've been delivered from that bondage, hallelujah.

I was out there mowing and rehearsing what she'd said to me and the more I thought about it, the angrier I got. The devil loved it and he started piping in my ear, *Why don't you just go on in there and give her a piece of your mind!*

I lifted my fists to the sky and said, "Yeah, I *would* like to give her a piece of these too!"

I tell you what, I heard his little voice say to my mind, *I think she treats you wrong.*

I said, "You know her, don't you?"

He said, *Yeah, I do.*

Man, my mind was flowing with all kinds of thoughts. The devil was just lying to me like a dog, and I knew it, but I was willing to listen to him for a little while! He was saying exactly what I wanted to hear and the more grass I cut, the more stirred up I got. "I tell you one thing," I said, "I should just go in there and…"

I'll go with you, he said. *I will stand with you. I am on your side. She deserves it.*

Boy, the devil knew how to stoke my fire! Why? He has studied human nature for millenniums. He knew I was raised as a Cajun boy. He knew that my Grandpa used to tell me, "If your wife tells you something you don't like, tell her to shut up." That is that old Cajun way. Men are the top dogs and women eat the scraps. Of course, Grandpa is dead today. And, well, he was a liar because Grandma ran the house. But when I was pushing that lawn mower, it didn't matter! I was ticked and ready to heap vengeance on my wife.

I stormed back into the house as mad as a hornet and started hollering, "Cathy, I want to tell you something!" She looked at me, pointed and said, "I rebuke you – you devil from Hell. Get out of here! Jesse, stay where you are."

Suddenly, the devil left me by myself…by myself! I didn't want him to go. I was right. She needed to hear what I had to say. But, suddenly, everything changed. I looked around for the devil and he was gone, man. He didn't stand by my side. He left me right in front of a Holy Ghost woman!

Cathy looked at me and kindly said, "Now, what do you want, honey?"

"Nothing. Not a thing. I don't want anything," and I walked back to the mower, defeated. I wasn't out there for more than thirty seconds before that devil popped up again. *What did she say?* he asked, as if he was angry and I ought to go back in there and say something.

"Shut up!" I told him, "Get out of here!" I broke the connection with that boy. I realized that I was a fool to listen to him. He never steers me right. But, God's Word always stands true.

Vengeance is the Lord's – Not Mine!

> *If it be possible, as much as lieth in you, live peaceably with all men.*
>
> *Dearly beloved, avenge not yourselves, but rather give place unto wrath: for it is written, Vengeance is mine; I will repay, saith the Lord.*
>
> *Therefore if thine enemy hunger, feed him; if he thirst, give him drink: for in so doing thou shalt heap coals of fire on his head.*
>
> *Be not overcome of evil, but overcome evil with good.*
>
> Romans 12:18-21

That word "men" in verse 18 includes women too. God has called us to live as peaceably as we can with other people. Why did He have to tell us that? Because He knew we'd be tempted to avenge ourselves and exercise our own wrath on people when we don't like what they're saying and doing. But, He called us to *"overcome evil with good."* That's easier said than done!

God wants to take care of situations that call for vengeance –

and He's the judge of when, where and how vengeance should occur. Not us!

Increase the Power of Good in the World and You Will Diminish the Force of Evil.

If you don't focus on evil and, instead, you focus on the power of doing good, evil will diminish as a result. As a Christian, you should focus on saying good things, doing good things and allowing God to help you resist the temptation to fall in line with the darkness of this world. The more you give your attention to the devil and what's bad in the world, the more your mind will go off track. So, switch your focus to what's good.

Focus on going to church. It's a good thing. Focus on forgiving people you can't stand. That's good too. Focus on giving, sowing mercy and living holy. Those are all good and they'll change the atmosphere around you. When your mindset is right, it's easier to do right.

If others are talking trash, change the subject to something good. Don't be a humorless Christian who is always berating somebody about sin. Nobody wants to be around browbeaters. Focus on having joy in your life, smiling at others and being a good example. The more you focus on what's good, the less you'll be tempted by what's evil.

Educate Yourself on Righteousness

If you are the righteousness of God, then you ought to do what is right, but it will always start in your heart. You can't succeed at living clean if you don't believe you can. You have to believe in God and His ability to give you strength.

Educate yourself on righteousness. That is one way you're going to gain strength. Let God show you what it really means to be righteous. What did the blood of Jesus do for you? How does that practically affect your life?

"For He hath made Him to be sin for us, who knew no sin; that we might be made the righteousness of God in Him" (2 Corinthians 5:21). God always does what is right, and He has called you the righteousness of God. The more you let the reality of what Jesus did at the cross sink into your mind, the more difficult it will be for the dirt to hang around.

> *Thou wilt keep him in perfect peace, whose mind is stayed on Thee: because he trusteth in Thee.*
> *Trust ye in the LORD for ever: for in the LORD JEHOVAH is everlasting strength.*
>
> Isaiah 26:3-4

The more you trust in God as your strength, the stronger you'll become. He will give your body and your mind an education! He'll make it difficult for dirt to survive, much less thrive! *"Say ye to the righteous, that it shall be well with him: for they shall eat the fruit of their doings"* (Isaiah 3:10).

God promises that if you do what's right, you'll eat the fruit of it – which is success with God and man. It pays to follow God!

Never Become the Slave of Your Enemy

You are the master of your own mind, your own body and your own life. If you're not ruling yourself, it's just because you relinquished control somewhere along the line. You aren't a slave to your own mind and body, and the sooner you realize that and take back control, the better off you'll be.

You don't have to war with your flesh. Temptations may come, but you can choose to live this life without constantly battling yourself. In the beginning, it's hard to resist temptation because you're not accustomed to it, but the more you resist, the stronger you get. Pretty soon, you'll get to be like Paul the Apostle who said, *"For though we walk in the flesh, we do not war after the flesh"* (2 Corinthians 10:3).

This is a great victory that you're going to experience, if you pursue Paul's advice: *"Casting down imaginations, and every high thing that exalteth itself against the knowledge of God, and bringing into captivity every thought to the obedience of Christ"* (2 Corinthians 10:5).

Paul came to a point in his life that he was not a slave to his own mind and body. He decided that he could master himself because of the work of Christ. Christ would help him resist. Christ would give him strength. Christ would help him to do the right thing, the good thing, and live up to his potential. He assisted Christ by bringing his thought-life under control.

Admit it, Quit it and Forget it!

I don't pander to people and, I guess, that's why God didn't give me the calling of a pastor. It's hard for me to sit there talking to somebody who has no intention of actually doing what God says to do. A friend of mine says he's got a three-point counseling method: "Admit it, quit it and forget it." That's about how I feel!

Once, a woman wanted me to counsel her and her husband. She said, "I have committed adultery."

I asked, "Why?"

She said, "I don't know."

I said, "You are lying. You know exactly why. Now, don't lie to me. Where is your husband?"

"He is outside," she said.

"Bring him in here," I said. Then, I asked the husband, "Did you commit adultery too?"

He said, "Yeah."

I said, "Why?"

He said, "I don't know."

I said, "Both of y'all are liars."

She said, "Brother Jesse, we have come to talk to you about it."

I said, "Get on your knees. I am going to cast the devil out of both of you right now." Well, they haven't been back. That means it was either a really bad session or a really good session. I don't know, but when it comes to dealing with sin, I don't sweat all the details. To me, it's just pointless to rehearse the problem once you know what it is. At that point, all you really need to do is repent – turn away from sin and develop the strength to not do it again.

If you've fallen, don't lie to yourself and give excuses for sin. There is no excuse that's good enough. People say, "But I was snared." I say, "Lie, you fry! People don't snare you; you're snared with the words of your own mouth. Look, if you knew it was wrong and you did it anyway, just repent. Stop trying to justify yourself. Just fall on the mercy and grace of God." (See Prov. 6:2)

Most people just need to make a decision to follow God and stop pandering to the flesh all the time. Sure, we're human and we mess up, but, at some point, we should mess up less and less. At some point, we should be able to be honest enough to say, "I blew it! Thank God for the blood! Jesus, forgive me!" Then, we should just go on, strengthen ourselves where we're weak and start doing right again.

Don't make excuses for your flesh. If you choose to reject Christ, don't pretend you're living clean. At least, be honest about it. If you're giving up on God, don't do it sitting in a pew. Go to Hell with gusto. Have as much fun as you can because, later, it's going to be literally Hell to pay if you don't repent. But, if you love God and you want to live right, then make it simple for yourself.

If you have a problem with lust and some fine looking person comes up to you and says, "What's happening?" Tell them, "Nothing – next statement." Close the book on them. Don't let the devil stroke your ego. Stop the situation before you give in to temptation. Open your eyes to the subtlety of Satan.

Sin
will charge
YOU *more*
than you want to pay...

The subtlety of Satan
The straight-forward power
of JESUS CHRIST

CHAPTER 6

The Subtlety of Satan

Satan is sneaky and subtle. He doesn't want to shock you. He wants to lure you into sin. That's why it's called "deception" and "temptation" – he is putting out bait to catch you off guard. When you aren't expecting it, he shows you something tempting. When you aren't expecting it, he tries to subtly turn your eyes towards forbidden fruit – to plant ideas in your head that go against the Word of God. That's why you've got to have your eyes wide open.

The devil began to work his subtle deception in the Garden of Eden. The Bible tells the story that Satan took on the form of a serpent and began chatting with Eve about God and forbidden fruit – subtly questioning her about truth and God's motives.

In Genesis 3:1 it says, *"Now the serpent was more subtle than any beast of the field which the LORD God had made. And he said, unto the woman, Yea, hath God said, Ye shall not eat of every tree of the garden?"* (Genesis 3:1).

Notice that the devil didn't immediately criticize God. Nothing was negative at first. Instead, the devil just questioned Eve about what God said. Of course, the devil already knew what God said but he asked Eve to repeat it so that he could subtly weave the conversation his way. He wanted to get her into a discussion about the forbidden fruit.

*And the woman said unto the serpent, We may eat of
the fruit of the trees of the garden:*

*But of the fruit of the tree which is in the midst of the
garden, God hath said, Ye shall not eat of it, neither
shall ye touch it, lest ye die.*

*And the serpent said unto the woman, Ye shall not
surely die*

Genesis 3:2-4

Now, the devil is basically mocking God by dismissing what He said. God told Eve she'd die. The serpent said she would not die. But, continuing in his subtlety, the devil gives Eve an explanation. He wants her to tap into the pride that she has in her own intellect. So, he tells her a "real" reason that God doesn't want her to eat the fruit – like its some big secret she's missing out on.

"For God doth know that in the day ye eat thereof, then your eyes shall be opened, and ye shall be as gods, knowing good and evil" (Genesis 3:5).

He's trying to engage even more pride on Eve's part. Wouldn't she like to be "as gods"? Wouldn't she like to know good and evil? What he was saying was, 'Don't you know that there is more to life than the trees you have?'

Convinced that she's missing out and that God lied to her, Eve looks at the tree. *"And when the woman saw that the tree was good for food..."* (Genesis 3:6). She noticed that the fruit appeared to be good for food.

That's how sin is, you know. The devil always makes it look good. Even Jesus said that it is pleasurable to sin. That's the lure of it. I like to say that, at first, being drunk is a whole lot of fun, but, by the end of the night, you're hugging a filthy toilet and feel like you're going to die!

It Starts With A Question

Why do people sin? Because it's pleasurable. There's no point to lie about it. Smoking dope is fun. Drugs feel good. That's why people do it. But, it's the effect that hurts you in the end. At first, it's just for fun and then, you find yourself relying on it to do something for you that you can't get on your own. The reality is that something *in* you is missing, and you're self-medicating to get rid of it.

Sin is fun, but it will take you further than you want to go. John 8:34 says, *"Jesus answered them, Verily, verily, I say unto you, Whosoever committeth sin is the servant of sin."* You end up being a slave to the very thing that you thought would make you feel good and free.

For Eve, the lure of the fruit was in its beauty. This tree *"...was pleasant to the eyes, and a tree to be desired to make one wise, she took of the fruit thereof, and did eat, and gave also unto her husband with her; and he did eat"* (Genesis 3:6). That day, sin came in a snake-like manner. It brought up a question, tempted the pride of intellect and lured with beauty. The end result was a world of death, sickness and misery – but it started out looking really good.

Sin always begins by putting a little question in your mind. *'What do you think about this?'* or *'Why don't you try that?'* or *'Why not do it? What's it really going to hurt?'* The devil never starts with an answer because he has no answer. He just wants to get you thinking outside of the goodness of God.

Don't Look At It or Consider It – Stay Shocked by Sin

I want you to notice that Eve never told the devil to shut up. She didn't seem shocked by the devil's words. She listened to what he had to say, and he steered her into questioning God's motives and looking, longingly, at sin.

She should have told him to take a hike. Instead, she just let the devil's voice fill her head up with questions and she looked at the fruit long enough to consider its taste.

People who fall into sin make that kind of mistake all the time. If you want to be safe from sin, don't look at it. Don't spend time staring at what's tempting or thinking about what it would be like to have it or do it.

In the Bible, Joseph did the right thing when his boss's wife dropped her clothes and flat out said, 'Come here boy. Me and you are going to have some fun today!' (Paraphrase of Genesis 39:7-16.)

Joseph didn't hang out and say, "Wow, woman! You look good!" No, instead he ran away. Why? Because he was shocked at sin and refused to stand there and gaze on the naked woman. He refused to stand there and gaze upon someone whom he had no business looking at.

Why did David commit adultery with Bathsheba? Because he didn't leave when he caught her taking a bath. He saw her, stopped and gazed at her. He thought about her. He wasn't shocked and he sure didn't run. So, unlike Joseph, he fell into sin with the woman. The security lies in being shocked enough by sin to run from it – not to stare at it.

I Will Not Hurt My God

One of the things I really like about Joseph is that he thought of
God and the woman's husband before he thought of his own flesh.
When Potiphar's wife told him to sleep with her, the Bible says,
*"But he refused, and said unto his master's wife, Behold, my master
wotteth not what is with me in the house, and he hath committed all
that he hath to my hand; There is none greater in this house than I;
neither hath he kept back any thing from me but thee, because thou
art his wife: how then can I do this great wickedness, and sin
against God?"* (Genesis 39:8-9)

Many men wouldn't have been able to turn down an offer for sex,
no matter if it was their boss's wife, but Joseph was honorable. He
saw deception for what it was and said, 'I can't do this to my God
and, besides, your husband has been so nice to me. I don't want to
hurt him neither.' Joseph knew that he wasn't alone with Potiphar's
wife that day. God was in the room with him and his inner tapping
told him to resist temptation.

It is good to have the realization that God is always with you.
He never turns His eyes away from you. If you go into a store and
decide to steal, don't bother to look around to see who is watching. Realize that God is watching. He's right there with you. He
never leaves you or forsakes you – whether you are doing good or
bad deeds. Choose to be honorable and concerned about God's
feelings like Joseph.

If some woman or man makes an advance towards you sexually,
just tell them, "I appreciate that you think I'm good looking, but
I've got Christ in my life. I don't want to hurt my God by doing

something I know is wrong. And, I'd hate to see you being used and abused either."

You don't have to make people feel like they're the scum of the earth because they're just living according to their feelings. They are probably just blind to the fact that there is a better life in being blameless before God. So, you never attack the person. If you want to attack something, attack the spirit motivating them to tempt you with something you know is a weakness.

> But every man is tempted, when he is drawn away of
> his own lust, and enticed.
> Then when lust hath conceived, it bringeth forth sin:
> and sin, when it is finished, bringeth forth death.
> Do not err, my beloved brethren.
>
> James 1:14-16

Distortion, Doubt and Denial

You "err" when you allow the devil to distort your view of God, to get you into doubt and to deny that God's Word is true. Remember, before the serpent started lying to Eve, she and Adam lived a good life. They simply believed what God said and everything was fine.

The devil stroked Eve's pride because he wanted to appeal to her human intellect – part of her flesh side. She had no sin in her life but she did have free will. Satan used what he thought would cause Eve to question God – her pride in her own mind and the beauty of the forbidden fruit. The devil is so prideful; he almost always begins his subtle tactics by stroking a person's pride.

When the devil comes to tempt you, he will usually pose questions in order to cast doubt in your mind. He will insinuate things about God and try to give you a distorted view of God. Then, like he did with Eve, he will show you the beauty of what lies on the other side of God's best. What is he doing? He's painting a distorted picture for you and the longer you gaze at his picture, the more likely you are to fall into the next phase – denial.

If you're in the gazing and contemplating process, you may find that Satan's distorted view starts to creep out of your mind and begins to come out of your mouth. It could be something that seems simple like, "God won't do what He said. Not for me. Maybe for someone else, but not for me." Why would you think that God is not good? What makes you think that He is not a loving God who wants only the best for you – whether that is a holy life, a healthy life or a prosperous life?

You shine a bright light on the subtlety of sin when you stop letting the devil's questioning remain in your mind. Don't let your mind run wild with thoughts that insinuate God isn't good. He is good! Read His Word and let His love for you fill your mind to overflowing, so that you can have faith in Him.

Strengthen Your Faith in God

Faith will begin in your heart when you hear the Word of God with your own ears – not just once, but over and over. Romans 10:17, *"So then faith cometh by hearing, and hearing by the word of God."*

"Heard" doesn't equal faith. "Hearing and hearing" equals faith! You have to ask yourself, "Will I believe God or the devil? Will I decide to live according to God's Word? Will I be faithful to my personal convictions?"

Commit to reading the Word of God for yourself and listening to messages that will build your faith. Commit to doing what He's told you to do and believing what He says, even if it goes against everything the devil tells you. That's what I've tried my best to do over my many years of knowing God and being in His ministry – and God has yet to steer me wrong.

When everybody said I couldn't live for God, God said I could. When everybody said I wouldn't be able to do what He said, God said I would. Do you know what I found out? God is right. He's always on target. And, as long as we keep our eye on His mark, we'll never miss it. We'll be able to detect the devil's lies and continue to walk in faith.

CHAPTER 7

You Can Overcome Anything

When I got saved, God not only washed away all my sin, but He also gave me a new outlook on life. He opened my eyes so that I could see myself as He sees me.

Salvation made me realize that I am more than just a bunch of body parts. I'm more than just a set of passed down genes. I am a spirit being, made in the very image of God, and there is nothing that is impossible for me if I "only believe."

I believe that the Apostle Paul felt the same way – but he said it in a different way. To Paul, accepting Christ's sacrifice was like dying to himself and being reborn through Jesus Christ. He identified with Christ so much that, to him, getting saved was sort of like being crucified on the cross with Jesus and dying to all the sinful ways of his old life. He said it this way.

> *I am crucified with Christ: nevertheless I live; yet not I, but Christ liveth in me: and the life which I now live in the flesh I live by the faith of the Son of God, who loved me, and gave Himself for me.*
>
> Galatians 2:20

Paul's old ways died when he accepted Jesus' sacrifice on the cross. He said, and this is my paraphrase, 'People, you're looking at a dead man! I've been crucified with Jesus. That person you knew before is gone. I'm new. I'm different. Jesus has saved me and now, He's the One who is living through me. My life is a life of faith! My faith is in the One who loved me enough to go to the cross and die for my sins – Jesus Christ. My flesh is dead to the old ways and my spirit is alive!'

Paul decided that he didn't have to cater to the desires of his old flesh like some animal roaming through the desert. He had climbed up a notch when he accepted Jesus. Of course, Paul was encased in a body of flesh and bone just like you and me. He had a mind, a will and a set of emotions just like we do. But, Paul realized that he was more than just the sum of his physical parts. He knew that he was a spirit being first, and the flesh he inhabited wasn't supposed to rule his life.

I've decided to adopt Paul's mentality and put myself in the scripture. I like to say, "I'm a dead man too! It's not Jesse that lives anymore; it's Christ who lives through Jesse. I'm living by my faith in the Son of God, who loved me enough to die for me. I'm not going back to where I was before. I'm a new creature with a new feature – alive in Christ and dead to my old way of living."

Your Body is Secondary, But Your Spirit is Eternal

A friend of mine often shares that when God breathed the breath of life into us, He created what she calls, "speaking spirits." We are spirit beings made in the very image of God, with the authority and the ability to rule over our own body.

The more you realize that you are a speaking spirit, made in the image of God and able to command your flesh to get in line, the more you'll understand that you don't have to be swayed by everything your physical body wants to do.

Your body will pull you to do all sorts of stuff! But you don't have to listen to it.

It's not the "the real you" anyway. One day, your body is going to die and return to the earth from which it came, but your spirit is going to live forever. Of course, the better you take care of your body, the longer you get to live in it. But, make no mistake, when it bites the dust, your reborn spirit is going to move to Heaven where you'll live in the presence of God for eternity. Think about that.

Get a revelation of yourself as eternal. When you do, you'll start to realize that it's just not right to let your physical body govern your life. It's wonderfully made and a gift of God to you, but it's secondary to your spirit.

I meet a lot of people who think that they have to obey every inclination of their flesh, but they don't. They operate their lives according to how they feel that day. If I obeyed my feelings and listened to my mind every time it said, *Eat that cake, Jesse.* I'd be nine hundred pounds! Sure, leftover chicken legs may call me in the middle of the night, but I don't listen to them. I crucify my flesh and leave the bird's legs alone at three in the morning!

Sinning Doesn't Happen in the Spirit

Sinning doesn't happen in the spirit; it happens in the flesh. So, if you crucify your flesh daily, instead of just on Sunday, you're going to be more successful at avoiding the subtlety of sin.

There is always going to be tug of war going on between your spirit and your flesh. Your fleshly body pulls on you to do whatever it wants to do and your spirit says, '*No, this is the best way. This is what the Lord says.*' So, you have a choice at that moment. The only time you can really sin is if you are in the flesh – if you've decided to do things your own way instead of His way.

If you wait until Sunday to fill-up on God, then you're going to be dry a lot of the time and far more vulnerable to the tug of your flesh. That's why committing your day to God first thing in the morning is a good idea. Praying everyday and taking time to put some of the Word into your mind is crucial.

It will just drive you nuts if you do your own thing all week long and then suddenly get spiritual on Sunday. That flip-flopping back and forth won't give you the strength, faith or character you need to avoid sin.

Hit and miss Christianity just doesn't produce the best results. The principles of God's Word work, but in order for your faith to be effective, you have to give God more than just one day a week to help you out!

It Isn't Just Fire Insurance

When Jesus came into my life, He delivered me from Hell and a hellish life. Once I made a decision to accept Jesus as my Savior, I felt there was no other option than to let Him be the leader of my life too. Why would I want to keep on doing things the old way? They were killing me! So, I accepted that God's way worked better than my way. There was nothing in my old life that I wanted anymore.

It's always amazing to me when I hear about a Christian who turns his back on God. I wonder, *Maybe they didn't get saved the way they should have. Man, when you see the glory of God, what does the world have to offer?* It amazes me that people would turn their back on God after years of being in the faith. Why would anyone deliberately choose to go back to a lost and dying world? I mean, what in Hell do they really want?

When I got saved, I wasn't just trying to purchase "fire insurance." I needed a complete turn around because the devil was beating my brains out. Sure, the life I lived before brought me a little happiness here and there, but, overall, it was doing nothing but dragging me further and further into a pit of emptiness, misery and pressure to succeed at whatever the cost. I had no true happiness and no true peace in my mind.

If you would have asked me, "What in Hell do you want?" when I got saved, I would have hollered, "NOTHING! I got a glimpse of Hell when I was living for the devil and I don't want anymore of it!" So, when I see that someone is getting away from God and reverting to their old lifestyle, I want to shake them and ask, "What in Hell do you want? What does Hell have to offer you? Don't let the devil lie to you and steal everything you've got, because if you let him, he will do it!"

Pluck it Out, Cut it Off!

If you give the devil a little place in your life, he will keep taking a little bit more. Before you know it, you'll be headlong into sin – sick, sad and disgusted about it, but too embarrassed to let anybody know about it.

The devil works on pride and there is nothing he has to offer you that comes without a steep price tag. Sin will always cost you something, but God will always give you something. I know that in the beginning, sin doesn't seem to cost too much, but in the end, sin will always charge you more than you ever wanted to pay.

Knowing that the devil steals but actually avoiding his thievery are two different things entirely. You can know something in your mind, but if you aren't willing to let it seep into your heart and change you, then nothing is going to get better.

God created you in His image and likeness and wants to see you overcome sin and become the strong person He created you to be in Him. If you're being tempted, I want you to know right now that it isn't God's will that you give in.

Jesus was adamant about teaching us how to walk upright and avoid sin. He said, *"And if thine eye offend thee, pluck it out, and cast it from thee: it is better for thee to enter into life with one eye, rather than having two eyes to be cast into hell fire"* (Matthew 18:9).

In other words, Jesus said, 'If you're struggling with something that is bringing you down into sin all the time, it's better for you to completely cut yourself off from it than to stay around it and fall again and again. It's better for you to cut yourself off from that sin and get into Heaven, rather than continue in that sin and burn in Hell.' (my paraphrase)

This parable isn't meaning that you should go around lopping off body parts! It's meant to show you the importance of doing everything you can to live right and avoid what makes you stumble at all costs. It's best just to pluck out the sin while you can and go about living the good life that God has destined for you to live.

Nobody is perfect and God will grant you grace and mercy at every turn, but Jesus wants you to aim at making sin a black-and-white issue – not a stumbling gray area. He wants you to develop a "what's right is right, and what's wrong is wrong" attitude when it comes to sin. The more you allow the devil to distort your view, the more gray area you'll get into and the more trouble you'll find yourself in too.

Choosing to Give it Up

The devil will usually try and get you to be compulsive or obsessive in some way. God doesn't want you to live like that – it's hellish! Any vice taking His place in your life is no good. But, thank God, *"From the Lord comes deliverance..."* (Psalm 3:8, NIV).

He'll help you, if you ask in faith, but He won't force Himself on you. If you want to resist the devil, He'll help you. You just have to make a clear-cut decision that it's what you really want. There is no need in playing games. Just ask yourself, "Why am I struggling with this? What do I really want? What does the devil have to offer me? Do I want to listen to his lies or follow the Lord Jesus instead?" Be honest with yourself. Make certain that you are serious about making a change in your life.

You don't have to worry about doing it on your own. Just admit to yourself that you need Jesus to help you resist sin, and He'll help you. He will tap your spirit as long as you ask Him to do it. He'll bring scripture back to your memory and give you the strength to say "no" when the devil comes with his devices.

It doesn't matter whether you're tempted with drugs, alcohol, pornography, adultery, gambling, food or anything else, you can overcome temptation. With God's help, you can overcome *anything* the devil throws your way.

CHAPTER 8

Dogs and Vomit, Fools and Follies

I've always been an extreme type of person. Before I came to the Lord, I wasn't your average sinner. I sinned as much as I could because I figured that this life was all there was; I might as well make the most of it.

I didn't realize that I was deceived and living low. Back then, I was strung out on drugs and drinking a minimum of a bottle of whiskey per day, playing rock music and going to Hell with gusto.

But, when I found out the truth and decided to give my life to the Lord Jesus, I didn't play games. God came into my heart and I decided to follow Him. I didn't struggle with any kind of withdrawal from the drugs or the booze; I was totally delivered. It was supernatural, I know, but it was also fueled by my desire to never go back to that old life.

Now, I didn't look any different. I didn't even smell different; but I was different! God had changed me on the inside and it affected what I did on the outside. I shared this with you so you'll realize how important it is to make a quality decision concerning addictions of any kind.

If you want to be delivered from something that has been giving you trouble in your Christian walk, you have to want to make Jesus more than your Savior – you have to make Him your Lord.

If you only allow Jesus to be your Savior, you're going to need a lot of rescuing in life! Why? Because you'll still be doing things your own way. Let's just face it, doing things your own way didn't work in the past, so it's obviously not going to work in the future.

Jesus will always be there to help you out of the ditches of life but why wade through a ditch when you can rise above it? Why wade knee-deep in mud when you can do the high-step on a clean and clear path?

Do You Have a Hard Time Sinning?

When Jesus is your Lord, you are not the kind of person who just reads the Word and does his own thing. You're the kind of person who reads the Word and applies it too. You allow your Lord to guide your steps in life. There is so much wisdom in the Bible; it's more than you'll ever need. It's a book of wisdom for living. So, when you read it and do what it says, its teachings can help you avoid the ditches of life.

Do you have a hard time sinning? When Jesus is your Lord, it just isn't easy to sin. Sin goes against everything you're living for, so when you're confronted with it, you notice it for what it is – deadly!

Sin becomes like a big hunk of juicy meat…that's rancid and stinks to high Heaven. You see it sitting on the plate and although others are tempted by it, you don't have the least inclination to take a bite. Instead, you just push yourself away from the table. If you happened to be deceived into taking a bite of that rancid meat for some reason, you immediately notice the rank stuff when it hits your mouth. Why? Because Jesus is your Lord and you're conditioned to live holy.

Why Would You Want To Go Back?

I could have gotten as drunk as a skunk the day after I got saved, if I wanted to. There was nothing physically holding me back from shooting up. What stopped me? My new found faith and my inner conviction to follow God and do right.

Although God had changed me, I had the power to go against His change in my life. Psalm 106:43 (NIV) illustrates this when it says, *"Many times He delivered them, but they were bent on rebellion and they wasted away in their sin."*

I didn't want to be rebellious anymore. I didn't want to waste away in my own sinful state. God had done too much for me to turn back. So, because I made the decision to turn away from my old life, I believe that God honored me and took away my compulsive and obsessive behaviors concerning alcohol and drugs. He did it the minute I gave the problem and my life to Him.

Sure, the devil came to tempt me later when I had been living for God for a little while and the "newness" of my conversion had faded, but because of my commitment to God daily (not just Sunday), I was able to resist the temptation and continue in my new life.

God can take away every compulsive desire and give you the strength to say "No!" He did it for me. He'll do it for you! When God is in your life, you have the power to resist the devil. When He is your Lord, you never want to go back to doing things the old way! Sure, you could sin anytime you want – but why you would want to?

Fools, Folly and Vomit-Eating Dogs

Do you know that the very night I gave my life to Jesus, I had a gig scheduled? People have asked me, "Did you go through with playing music that night, Brother Jesse?"

Yeah, I did. I was under contract to play music that night, and I had a job to do – so, I did it. But I'd changed inside and my eyes were opened. I looked around the club I was playing and saw a velvet sewer. You see, before I was saved, those places looked good to me. They were fun. Once I was saved, they looked like red velvet sewers and I didn't want any part of them. The Bible has a different way of describing what it's like to go back to a life of sin, and it includes vomit and dogs.

Have you ever seen a dog throw up and then go back and eat it? It'll make you fast for days! There is hardly anything more disgusting than having to look at that! Yet, that's exactly what the Bible says you are like when you go right back to the stuff that messed you up in the first place. *"As a dog returneth to his vomit, so a fool returneth to his folly"* (Proverbs 26:11).

That word "folly" is just another word for stupid trouble which means, if you *keep* doing what gets you into trouble, you're like a dumb dog that goes back and eats his own vomit. Now, that's just plain disgusting. On top of that, it's just plain foolish.

It's foolish to entertain the lies the devil throws into your head. He's a loser. He's going to Hell. It's foolish to listen to his lies and doubt God – the One who made the universe and everything in it. The Bible says that a fool says in his heart that there is no God. (See Psalm 14:1)

I think I'd have a hard time backsliding because I just don't like vomit, I don't want to be compared to a dumb dog and I don't enjoy the idea that rejecting God means siding with the devil – and that leads to a fiery pit. I have to tell you, I don't enjoy the idea of being burned. I don't look back at my old life and miss it. The bottom line is that there is nothing in Hell that I want; there is really no place for me to go back to.

Spiritualized Common Sense

I find that when you're dealing with the things of God, some people throw their common sense out the window. I don't believe that's a good thing to do. God gave you common sense for a reason, and when you get born again, you just start spiritualizing your common sense. You decide in your heart that the Word is true and that God's thoughts and ways are higher than yours.

God knows what He's talking about. He made you and He knows how slick the devil can be. His Word is there to help you out in life and give you wisdom – so you don't keep going back to the vomit of a sinful life. God is perpetually reaching out to you. He wants to communicate with you and give you His wisdom.

Before you were born again, you used your common sense to get through life. After you're born again, you can use your spiritualized common sense to see through the eyes of faith and say, "That's what God said, so I believe it." Even if reality seems to go against God's Word, spiritualized common sense says, "God said it, so who am I to argue. He knows what He's talking about!"

When the devil hits you with temptation, you use your spiritualized common sense and say, *'Now, devil you're going to have to bother somebody else with this temptation, because I'm no fool and I'm no dog! I ain't eating what you're throwing up, devil!'*

Confusing the Devil With His Own Confusion

The devil has tried to tempt me many times in my life, sometimes just by throwing doubt into my mind and confusing me about living for God. But I've figured out that I'm more powerful than that idiot. He's just a spiritually dead devil but I'm alive with the Spirit of God. I'm not some animal that is swayed by everything life throws my way. I am fulfilling my own destiny by simply sticking with God.

When the devil tempts me, I like to confuse the idiot with his own confusion. When he puts something in front of my eyes and whispers, *'Go ahead, Jesse, sin. You know you want to.'* I say, "No, way, devil! *You* sin!" The Bible says Satan is the author of confusion – so the boy is flat confused! If you asked him, "Well, Satan, what in Hell do I want?" He'll go, *'Nothing.'* He knows there is nothing in Hell that you really want. There's nothing in Hell that the devil wants either.

If you asked him, "Why would you ever think you could win against God, *you* stupid devil? Man, what in Hell do you want?" He'd go, *'I dunno.'* He's been fighting so long, he's confused about it! The devil is the biggest loser I know.

He's fighting a battle that has an ending that has already been written. The whole scenario of his finality is in the Word, but the devil is so confused about the whole situation that he just keeps on fighting hoping that one day something will change and he'll win his battle against God. He's a confused devil.

The devil has been away from God for so long, and every minute since he fell, he's been getting more and more confused. Why would he ever rebel against such a loving and giving God? Why would he start a war with His Maker? Because he has lost his senses. He's in love with himself. He's living in a whirlwind of pride and rebellion and it has blurred his vision. He can't see reality and he doesn't have spiritualized common sense.

Faith Doesn't Mean Much to the Devil

The devil is a flesh devil and so, that's the realm in which he operates. You'll throw him off guard by moving in the Spirit and speaking the Word.

Never attack the devil in the flesh. He'll kick your brains out if you do, because he has a lot of experience working in the flesh – he's been working his deception since the Garden of Eden. It worked on the first two people, so he's been doing the same thing ever since!

The five senses are something the boy understands. Human frailty is something he has a firm grasp on, and he'll try and manipulate you anyway he can. His understanding of the way the unrenewed mind works is his advantage when he's trying to tempt you or hinder you in life.

But, when it comes down to it, he's still just a flesh devil. He's not spiritually alive like you are and that puts him at a disadvantage. The devil doesn't believe anything by faith. He believes something when he sees it or when he sees it starting to happen.

When I said, "I'm going on television," the devil didn't believe it. I said it when I first started out in ministry, when my offerings were two dollars or a Dr. Pepper. I didn't have enough money for gas to make it back home, so the devil didn't believe for a second that I would ever be able to preach the Gospel on television. But, I did. I knew it was going to happen. I had faith, but the devil didn't. It wasn't until he saw me sign the contracts that he looked around at his imp buddies and said, *'Hey, he really is going on television!'* Then, he started trying to fight me about it and steal from me.

Have you ever noticed that the devil fights you when you get something from God? He doesn't bother you as much when you're using your faith. But when you actually start seeing your faith bring that miracle or blessing into existence, well, that's when he tries to rip you off! Do you know why? Because when you were speaking it by faith, the devil couldn't see it. And until he can see it, he doesn't fight it too much. When my television program became more than a prayer, that's when he fought me. That's when he said, *'Wow man, they are getting this thing. We've got to stop them. Throw this problem at them, throw that too!'*

So, when it comes to sin and temptation, if we don't live in the flesh, then we won't fulfill the lusts of the flesh. If we put our spirit in charge and let what we believe come before what we feel, the devil doesn't stand a chance at getting us to fall into sin.

Sin won't ask *for very much...*
in the beginning

But in the end?

It will
take everything you've got

The Lure of Temptation
The Power of Sanctification

CHAPTER 9

Temptation – Enduring It, Instead of Enjoying It

Have you ever noticed that the day you go on a protein diet is the day somebody offers you a slice of your favorite cake? Or, maybe you just decided to give up eating fatty foods, and that night, your spouse brings home fried chicken and onion rings for dinner? Those are temptations that are common to you! *"There hath no temptation taken you but such as is common to man..."* (1 Corinthians 10:13).

Everybody deals with the same few things. For you, it might be cake. If so, you know that you love cake! You'd give your right arm for a piece of cake when all you've eaten is raw broccoli and cauliflower all day!

That's where you've got to ask yourself, "What is a common temptation for me? What pulls on my flesh that I know isn't of God, and what makes me want to backslide?" Whatever you answer is what the devil will try and use to tempt you.

What's "Common" to Man

When someone tells me, "Brother Jesse, the temptation was so strong, I just couldn't refuse it," I know they're lying. While temptation may seem like it's overwhelming, the Bible says different.

"There hath no temptation taken you but such as is common to man: but God is faithful, who will not suffer you to be tempted above that ye are able; but will with the temptation also make a way to escape, that ye may be able to bear it" (1 Corinthians 10:13).

James 1:12 says, *"Blessed is the man that endureth temptation: for when he is tried, he shall receive the crown of life, which the Lord hath promised to them that love him."*

I see men my age that are looking to trade their fifty-year-old wife in for a twenty-five-year-old. They're tempted by that, and they enjoy the temptation. Man, I don't care how pretty another woman is, I don't want her! My wife is enough! Two of them with an American Express credit card would kill me! I don't want any more of that. I'm not crazy! The scripture doesn't say, "Blessed is the man that enjoyeth temptation" – it says you're blessed if you endure it!

There has been so many preachers and Christians falling into temptation. The media loves a good story, and I remember in the 1980s when preachers were falling like dominos and the world watched it on prime-time news.

In those days, I heard many that said things like, "I couldn't help myself" or "I was snared" or "The devil was so strong, I just couldn't resist." But, according to those scriptures above, God always makes a way of escape for people.

You see, if you know that the devil can only tempt you with what is "common to man" and you know that he is going to try and hit you in an area you're weaker in, then you can't be "snared." It's impossible. You already know what the devil is going to do.

The problem is that a lot of those who have fallen didn't really want to escape temptation, and they didn't want to take responsibility for what they did either. They preferred to make excuses and give in. Some had been giving in to temptation and sinning for years, but I believe the problem began because they didn't deal with their thought-life for years before. The battlefield is the mind.

They didn't have to remain transfixed by impure thoughts. They could have gone to God about it and let Him heal or deliver them from the root issue – because there is always a root issue when a sin is repetitive. And, it wouldn't have hurt them to get some private counseling with another minister to let the secret thoughts out.

Keeping Secrets Destroys Lives

Keeping secrets inside can be devastating and talking to another minister, who is older in the faith, can be what a person needs to get back on the right track. Accountability like that does wonders.

Sometimes it is enough to say it out loud to someone – to admit there is a problem. Sometimes that is enough for a person to wake up and say, "Man, what am I doing? I'm toying with this thing and there is so much to lose! Devil, you aren't stealing anything from me! I'm getting this root dug out and I'm starting on it today!" But, when the devil has a person over the barrel with a temptation, it may take more than that. It may take personal accountability to someone – a spouse, a friend, a minister or a counselor.

"How Could That Happen, Brother Jesse?"

When the first ministers in the 1980s started being exposed for their sin, it seemed like everywhere I went people asked me, "How could a minister of the Gospel give into temptation over and over again and still go out and preach?" At that time, I didn't know what to tell them. I'd done my sinning when I was a sinner, and I wasn't harboring or entertaining thoughts of going back into it. So, I'd just chime in with them and ask some of the same types of questions.

"Yeah," I'd say, "What do they do when they're getting in bed with another woman? Ask God to wait outside? Man, God sees everything!" It was almost a joke to me. How could anybody think they were able to hide their sin from God? Man, there are enough warnings in the Bible for this that I couldn't believe a strong, powerful and anointed minister of the Gospel could actually want to do this – or believe they wouldn't get caught in the sin!

But, it didn't take long for me to realize that maybe these men had been sinning in their mind long before they sinned with their body. They'd been making excuses in their mind for giving into temptation for years. Perhaps they had unholy ambition too and thought that they were so big in the Christian world that nothing could tear them down.

Believing the Devil's Lies

You see, the more a person thinks about sin, the easier it is to give in. The more they give in, the easier it is to keep giving in. Then, because a Christian's conscience can't handle it, they start to believe the lies of the devil and start to make excuses for sinning. They justify the sin in their own mind.

I'm sure that the very first time one of those ministers gave in to temptation and sinned, they were emotionally torn up about it. They probably asked for forgiveness from God and tried to never do it again. But, once a person gives in, the devil comes like a flood to tempt them over and over again.

The devil assaults the mind and tries to weaken the will of a person. If that person has only asked for forgiveness, but hasn't truly repented – meaning they haven't made a firm decision to turn away from the sin and begin to allow God to reveal and remove the root problem – they will most likely fall again. They'll begin to give into the temptation, and then, the excuses come rolling in. It's called denial or refusal to admit any fault.

That's why you saw some break so hard when they got caught. These men knew God, loved God and wanted to do right but they let the devil steal, kill and destroy their lives. They let their own egos get in the way and instead of enduring temptation, they relaxed into enjoyment mode. That's a scary place to be, especially if God has given you a place of high position in His ministry.

When the reality of what they had done hit them, I was shocked that some were so indignant while others were truly distraught. People sneered in the 1980s and said, "Oh, they're not sorry, they're just sorry they got caught!" I thought the same thing, and maybe in the beginning, that was true, but I think many people who fell into sin during this time became very sorry that they'd never dealt with the root issues before. I believe that, over time, they became very sorry that they'd brought the integrity of the Gospel down ten notches just by their notoriety as men of God.

Sin will always take you further than you want to go. It'll keep you longer than you want to stay, and it will charge you more than you want to pay. Sin took almost everything those preachers had –

their peace of mind, their marriages and their ministries. Sin even stole their divine destiny. Can you imagine where these men of God would be today had sin not stolen from them?

Can you imagine where *you* would be if you hadn't let the devil steal from you at different points in your life?

Learn from Other's Mistakes

The Bible is full of stories, as well as straight-up teaching. Some of the stories are victory stories and others are of people who have experienced the killing, stealing and life-destroying tactics of the devil. But, there is hope throughout the entire book that God will forgive and restore the life of anyone who calls on His name.

If you have fallen into sin, remember that while people may never forgive or forget your past, God will. He will be faithful to pick you up, clean you out and make you righteous and holy again.

The blood of Jesus is strong enough to cover any and every sin – even marriage-busting and ministry-stealing sin! No sin is too bad for His blood to wash away.

Recognizing When Somebody Has Been Redeemed

If you are living holy before God, it will sometimes be hard not to judge those who are falling into sin. It's natural to want to point out their every flaw, but it's not godly.

When we see somebody sin and then they repent, it's not our job to keep holding the sin over their head and reminding them of it. Our job as fellow believers is to recognize that they've struggled and pray for them. It's our job to recognize the redeeming power of the blood. Sure, we can see what they did and recognize the ways in which they went wrong so that we can learn from their mistakes, but we shouldn't condemn them. It's only pride that enjoys seeing someone else fall.

I'll never forget the day when I was on an airplane flying to preach a meeting right after a well-known preacher was accused in the media of committing adultery.

I was reading my Bible and this man sitting near me noticed. The Holy Spirit spoke up within me and warned me that I was about to be questioned.

"Are you a preacher?" I heard the man say.

"Yes sir." I said, and thought, *Here it comes. I am a television evangelist. Here it comes.* That well-known preacher had just been caught in sin and it was all over the news, papers and radio shows. You couldn't go anywhere without hearing about it. To say the word evangelist was like saying that fallen minister's name.

"Well," the man sneered and cocked back his head, "What do you think about that preacher's sin?" His face was all contorted with disgust.

You know how it is when you're on an airplane. Everybody can hear everything and when the man said that, everybody's ears perked up. They wanted to hear my reply. I looked him square in the face and decided not to whisper.

"Well, let's talk about your sin for ten minutes and then we are going to talk about his sin. Now, let me ask you, mister. Have you ever committed adultery?"

Now, when you say adultery, everybody looks at you. It

shocked the man!

"What?"

"Wait a minute," I said, "We are going to talk about that preacher's sin in a minute, but let's talk about yours first. Have you ever committed adultery? Come on, mister. Tell me. Have you done it?" I was getting loud. "Have you?" I asked again. He was just looking at me dumbfounded.

He started stumbling over his own lips, saying, "Uhhh. Uhhh." That's when his wife spoke up, "Well! Tell the man."

I chimed in, "Come on mister. Have you committed adultery? Tell me if you did."

"Tell the man!" his wife started lashing out, "Tell him!"

The man was speechless. I mean, he was trying to get something out, but all that came out was, "Argh, argh, uhh, argh…" The boy sounded like a seal. He never answered me. As he was walking off the plane, his wife was behind him and kept asking, "Did you? Did you? Did you?" Just getting all over him! As people filtered out, some said, "I bet he did it" and "You know he did it." People are something else, man!

You know, we never got past his sin, so we never had to talk about the preacher's sin. I left the names out, but I mentioned the story anyway because I want to get a point across – never attack someone that has asked for forgiveness. You might need forgiveness for yourself one day, and you don't want to be barking like a seal when somebody asks you about it! So, resist the urge to gloat and don't stick your foot in your mouth in the first place!

Remember, what people do may be wrong. You may have done some wrong things too. But, if God loves you enough to forgive you, the least others can do is agree that you're forgiven and stop dragging you over the coals! I believe we've got to love people even though they make mistakes, because a religion without love is a religion without power. And, we need all the power we can get to combat temptation and live victoriously in this life.

Thoughts

don't have to torment or

control you

YOU

can control your thoughts

The Battle of the Mind

The Victory of the Word

CHAPTER 10

Your Mind and Your Mouth –
Combating Thoughts

You may not be able to control what comes into your mind, but you can sure control what stays in there. Crazy thoughts can fly into your mind, but it's you who will decide what you will allow to hang around in your mind.

So, what do you do when thoughts that are NOT true, honest, pure, lovely, of good report, virtuous or worthy of praise come flying into your head? You combat them with the Word. You stop the thought before you get comfortable with it.

Some people figure that unseemly thoughts don't really do any harm. If they're not actually following through with what they're dreaming about, they assume it's OK. But, continually thinking wrong thoughts just leads to problems down the road and it makes you dissatisfied with where you are right now. It steals your peace.

I've had people tell me, "Brother Jesse, I can't stop thinking about this!" I say, "Yes you can! You may not be able to control the thought that comes in, but you can get rid of it."

Thoughts don't have to torment or control you. You can control your thoughts.

Do you know why I know you can? Because the Bible instructs you about *"...bringing into captivity every thought to the obedience of Christ"* (2 Corinthians 10:5). God wouldn't tell you to stop it in its tracks if He didn't know that you were capable of doing it.

The Mind and the Mouth

What do you use to combat thoughts? Words! Words are stronger than thoughts. If you start talking, your mind will shut up to hear what your mouth has to say.

If you don't believe it, try counting money *in your head* while someone yells different numbers. You'll lose track and will forget where you were in the counting. I've done that at banks before. The teller may be counting out money silently and I'll just start saying, "Five, six, seven, eight, nine, thirty-two, forty-five, ninety-eight..." They lose track every time! Do you know why? Because their mind will stop to listen to my words. They can't help it! The mind is made to *process* information. The mouth is made to *give* information.

Do you know how I handle big temptation? If a crazy thought comes whirling into my mind, I start talking to myself. Thoughts can be rough. When temptation is strong, it can get to the point that the tempting thoughts are controlling my mind. So, I've got do something more than just think nice thoughts. I've got to start talking to myself and saying things like, "Would Jesus do this today?" The moment I start talking, my mind stops to listen.

If you're being bombarded with all sorts of evil thoughts, guard yourself with your mouth. Don't acknowledge the thought as your own. It's not your thought, it's a tempting thought. So, say out loud, "That is not my thought! My thoughts are pure, lovely, virtuous, true, honest, of good report and full of praise. (See Philippians 4:8)

Reword the scriptures to include yourself so that they build you up. If the devil comes at your mind, talk to the boy! Say something like, "I will not think on those things, devil. You can't get one over on me, you lying devil!"

That's what I do, and it works. I just start encouraging myself in what the Word says about me. I'll say, "I am more than a conqueror. I'm strong in the Lord and the power of His might! I am an imitator of God, a recreated being. Old things have passed away from me and all things have become new for me! I am a spirit and I have the fruit of the Spirit operating in my life. I was chosen in Him before the creation of the world to be holy and blameless in His sight and that's what I am. I am an instrument for noble purposes, holy and useful to the Master, prepared for any good work! I am led by the Spirit of God, and I walk after the Spirit and not the flesh!"

The more I speak the Word, the more my faith rises. I may start out feeling weak and tempted, but once I begin talking and quoting the Word, I feel stronger. My mind clears. It's how I resist temptation, and it's not a hard thing to do. The more I combat thoughts with words, the more determined my faith gets. This will work for you too. It will work in any situation and with every temptation. You can regain control of your mind this way.

Start proclaiming. Even if your temptation is just something as seemingly innocent as gluttony, tell your body, "I know you're screaming at me for pizza, but I am not giving in because greater is He that is in me! I can do all things through Christ which strengtheneth me – and that includes self-control!"

If you start talking to yourself like that, you'll start feeling your power. You have to build yourself up. If you don't do it, who will? Look, it feels good to resist temptation. It feels good to know that your spirit is controlling your body, instead of the other way around. It feels right because it is right, and if you keep it up, pretty soon, it starts looking alright too!

If you just sit there and let your mind take over, you'll have visions of moon-pies and Krispy Kreme donuts…and you're going to crack! But, if you start talking and start defying what you're thinking, resisting temptation will start to get easy. You'll go long, extended periods of time without messing up.

Going Long Times Without Messing Up!

You'll get to a place where you've gotten "in Christ" when it comes to that temptation. You're flowing in His way instead of your way, saying what He says instead of what you would say and doing what He does instead of what you would do. Before you know it, you are what He says – victorious over the sin that once held you down!

The bottom line is that you believe what you say more than you believe what anybody else says! If you say what God says, then you'll start having more faith in Him. And it's your faith in God that makes such a huge difference in your life. Faith only increases one way. *"So then faith cometh by hearing, and hearing by the word of God"* (Romans 10:17). When you're talking faith and listening to yourself, well, that's a powerful combination!

The devil doesn't know what to do when you speak the Word of God over your life like that. He has nothing to fight with that compares to the sword of the Spirit. You can just cut his guts out with the Word and he eventually leaves because there is nothing more he can do.

Jesus knew this and that's why when He was tempted, He just used the Word. Read Luke chapter four and you'll see exactly how Jesus fought temptation. Eventually, the devil got tired of trying to get Jesus to fall into sin, and the boy left! Jesus wore him out so much that verse thirteen says the devil *"...departed from Him for a season."* Some time had to pass before the devil would come back to bother Jesus again!

I've had the devil leave me alone for a while too when it comes to temptation. Sometimes long periods of time go by without any temptation at all. Then he'll sneak up and try and tempt me again. You'll notice that the more you resist temptation, the easier it is to keep on resisting.

That rat won't leave forever, but once you understand the system and apply the scriptures, you know what you have to do to be successful in resisting him. It's called putting your spirit first place and your flesh last place. Of course, that takes effort. It's not something that just happens. It's a whole lot easier to get in the flesh. Do you know why? Because you've got more practice being in the flesh.

It's Easy to Get In the Flesh

I'll admit, there are times that I don't want to talk myself out of a temptation, especially when it comes to anger. I am a Cajun from South Louisiana and sometimes I get what we call "faché." That's Cajun slang word for being so ticked off that you want to slap somebody!

If you ever hear a Cajun say he's getting faché, just leave. Get out of the way because that guy is about ready to hit you. You've got to understand something; we've got Tabasco sauce running through our veins down here in South Louisiana! We've been eating crab boil and cayenne pepper since we were born, so we can get flat hot.

I had a really bad temper for years. Today, my patience is much stronger, but there was a time when I would get hot under the collar and snap at the drop of a hat. Today, it takes a lot longer, but I still lose it every now and then and have to repent!

If somebody gets in my face and says something I don't like, the Tabasco sauce rises up in my veins and I find myself wanting to say, "Uh, do you want some of me, Jack? I'll take this boot I'm wearing and put it where it hurts! Don't worry about it, I believe in healing and I'll pray for you later, but I'm going to kick you from here to the moon right now!"

I want to say that, but I catch myself. Before I was saved, I wouldn't have thought twice about saying it and adding a few cussing words along with my fist, but I am a new creature in Christ today! You see, even though I am saved, my flesh is weak. Sometimes, this flesh of mine will try getting off the cross and whipping up on a few people – it's called rebellion. So, I've got to take dominion over myself. I've got to put my flesh down, speak the Word to myself and shift over to the spirit!

I've got to start talking to myself from the right perspective and start saying the right things so that my mind will stop flooding me with the wrong things. I've got to start casting down imaginations that exalt themselves over the knowledge of God.

When anger rises up and I want to pop, I remind myself that Jesus never told me I couldn't get angry. He said, *"Be ye angry, and sin not: let not the sun go down upon your wrath: Neither give place to the devil"* (Eph. 4:26-27). How can I do that? By not yielding to my natural impulse.

"Can't He Drive the Car?"

I'll never forget when I was a baby Christian and I was driving in my car somewhere in a hurry. There was this guy driving in front of me and he was going so slow. I tried to pass him, but something would always happen and I couldn't make the pass. Either he'd speed up just enough to be side by side with the car in the other lane or I'd get over into the other lane and the car ahead of me would slow down even more. Man, I just couldn't pass the slow car up. So, I started talking to the driver from my car.

"What's the matter with this fool? Can't he drive the car?" Of course, he couldn't hear me, but I didn't stop griping about his driving! So, I thought to myself, I'm going to pass this joker, and when I get on the side of him I'm going to give him a piece of my mind.

Man, I was practically chewing the steering wheel by the time I got the chance to switch lanes, and speed up alongside of him. But, instead of making the pass when I wanted to, I found that I had to slow down because there was a traffic light ahead and it was changing to red. Of course, he was going so slow that he didn't bother running it. He stopped before the light even turned red. That's about when I slid up beside him, turned my face towards his window and noticed...he was my pastor!

He was already rolling down the window for me, but and I started stuttering. I pretended it was tongues and then said, "Oh, glory to

God. How are you doing, Pastor? Hobohabolobohobo..." It was one of those fake tongues like "Shama, shama, shama." Man, I was flat embarrassed.

"Was I driving slow?" he asked.

"Ummm, no." I lied like a dog! That made two sins I had to repent over.

"I just bought this car," he said, "and I can't figure out where everything is."

The light turned and he went along his way. I felt like a vomit-eating dog, returning back to the silly stuff I used to always do before I got saved!

Your Flesh Will Sin If You Don't Stop It!

You see, if you don't watch it, your flesh will try and sin on you. It'll do what it wants at the drop of hat. One minute you can be worshiping God in church and the next minute you can be screaming in the parking lot! How many times have you walked out of a Holy Ghost anointed, knockdown, power-packed service and gotten into your car with your wife – and started having a big fight. She says something that makes you mad or vice versa. You look at her and say, "Woman, I tell you one thing...!"

Or, you are driving out of the church parking lot and somebody cuts you off and then goes really slow. You just had a glorious anointed service and all of a sudden you're hollering out of the window, "Hey, if you can't drive the car, park it, man!" Does that sound familiar?

"When you're on TV, you've got to be nice all the time."

Preachers aren't any different when it comes to getting irritated or angry. We've got to crucify our flesh everyday too.

A while back I was talking with a couple who have been ministering the Word together for more than thirty years. They're on television all over the world. We were talking about it one day and she said, "You know, when you are on television as much as we are, you've got to be nice all the time." I laughed inside at that one because it's the truth. But, it's just not easy to be nice all the time!

When I get into a very uncomfortable situation and I feel like I'm about to lose it, I think to myself, "I am exercising my patience today!" I love people, and people love me, but sometimes there are situations that come up when you just don't want to talk – like a public bathroom for instance.

There have been times when all I want to do is use the bathroom, but somebody sees me go in the door and they follow me. They look under the stall doors to see if they can recognize my shoes and if they do, they jump into the stall right next to me and want to talk. They want me to crack jokes or something, but all I'm trying to do is use the throne! And I'd like to do it without talking to anybody but...

"Oh, Brother Jesse? You are Jesse Duplantis, right?"

"Yes."

"Oh! How are you doing? Oh, I guess you got..."

"Listen," I break in, "I've got to go to the bathroom."

"I'll go with you."

"No, no, I don't want you to go with me."

"Oh, but this is the only way I am going to get to talk to you."

I think to myself, *'Well, I guess I ain't going to the bathroom then.'* But, what I end up saying is, "What is your question?"

Do I want to be nice? No! I want to tell them to stop talking to me, get out the bathroom stall next to me, leave me alone and don't tell anybody you saw me! It's embarrassing!

Making the Effort to Do Right

Sure, you make an effort to do right every day. You do your best to follow what the Word says and not to make a fool of yourself – returning to your old ways like a dog returning to his own vomit. But, if you mess up and lap up a little of the gross stuff, all you've got to do is spit it out!

Ask for forgiveness. If you've totally blown it and you just can't convince yourself to do the right thing right away, don't just let the situation slide by without saying something. Come back later and ask for forgiveness once you've cooled down a bit – and here's the tough part, forgive the other person.

If you ask God for forgiveness from God for messing up but you're not willing to forgive the person who ticked you off in the first place, you're up a creek without a paddle. You have to forgive if you want God to forgive you. That's just the way things work.

Spiritual DNA

When I was a baby Christian, I used to make excuses for my

temper. I think I enjoyed indulging in it. But, today I know that there is no excuse for that. There are "generational curses," but Jesus redeemed us from the curse. So, if I hold on to a trait that is "in my family" I'm doing it by choice. The same is true for you.

Don't deceive yourself and think you can't change or that something is just in your family and it's just the way you are. You're saved, so you're free from the curse. Now, you've just got to realize it and ask God to help you break those habits that you've got in place.

My habit has always been to snap when I'm angry; everybody in my family does it, but that doesn't make it right! That doesn't make it acceptable, excusable and it's just a sad fact that my family found it enjoyable. If I just agree with them and say, "Well, that's the way we are" then I'm making an excuse to hold onto the family baggage. I can do anything I want to do. It isn't fun or easy, but I can do it.

Do you know how it all starts? When you are a little child and hear, "You're just like your Mama!" or "You're just like your Daddy!" Most of the time, kids hear that only when they're doing something wrong and it just keeps on enforcing the problem. If you hear that for long enough, you'll believe it to such a degree that it is an excuse for being the way that you are. What is that? Deception!

God made your spiritual DNA and it's good. You are good. If you want to get rid of a negative family trait that tempts you to sin, you can work it out of your personality. If you'll stop being deceived and start disciplining yourself to believe what God says about you, you'll start acting more like Him and less like "them."

Forget the negative stuff "they" said about you! Listen to what God says instead. He's only got good things to say about you.

CHAPTER 11

From Old Ways to ReNEWed Ways – Combating Lust

When God created man, His original plan was that the spirit would rule the soul (mind, will and emotions), and the soul would rule the body. When our spirit, soul, and body are in agreement, we have peace. God's plan for us is peace.

When man chose to disobey God and side with Satan, he lost his innocence and took on a sinful nature. Before the fall, man only knew good and he easily communicated with God. His spirit ruled as number one. After the fall, he came to know evil and this knowledge really changed his way of thinking, talking and living. That sin stood like a wall between man and God and it inhibited man from freely communicating with God.

Do you remember that God told man that if he ate of the tree of the knowledge of good and evil he would *die*? As you know, that death wasn't a natural death, it was a spiritual death. Once man couldn't talk to God, his spirit was as good as dead. So, mankind immediately began relying on his soul (mind, will and emotions) to govern his life – and because he no longer had God's influence, he became more and more "natural" in his thinking, talking and living.

Your spirit was created to hear God's voice, so when you accept Jesus, you can freely communicate with the Lord. After salvation, you're instructed in the Word to *"...be transformed by the renewing of your mind"* (Romans 12:2) and to *"...take every thought captive..."* (2 Corinthians 10:5).

You're not helpless or hopeless.

The mind is the battlefield and the enemy is fighting to keep every inch of territory. He doesn't give up easily! But, you have mighty weapons with which to fight him.

> *The weapons of our warfare are not carnal, but mighty through God to the pulling down of strongholds.*
>
> 2 Corinthians 10:4

We have to know who the Word says that we are, what the Word says we can become, and what the Word says we can do! We have authority over the enemy, but unless we realize it and exercise that authority, the enemy will rule over us.

This means that just because you're saved, your mind doesn't suddenly think God's way. You've got years of living "naturally" or without God's influence under your belt!

Now, once you know God, you begin on a journey to become more like Him – to allow His influence to change your way of thinking, talking and, ultimately, acting. Your goal is to renew your mind with the Word so that you not only think about what God says, but you believe His Word in your heart and say it with your mouth – that's what changes things.

Psalm 39:3 may give you some insight about dealing with the flesh. It says, *"My heart was hot within me; while I was musing, the fire burned: then I spoke with my tongue."*

In other words, as a human being, you either think, feel or say before you actually do something. Everything begins in the mind, and if you think about something long enough, you'll have some sort of emotional response concerning the object of your thoughts.

If you "muse" or meditate on something as this verse says, the thoughts will start to "burn" within you...if you get what I'm saying! Then, you may begin to speak about it and, ultimately, decide to act on what you've been thinking and talking about.

Lust – A Mind/Body Problem

Lust is a mind problem. If you're struggling with it and you want to get rid of it, the first step is to take control of it at the thought level like I mentioned in the last chapter. Don't allow the thought to tumble around in your mind. Don't meditate on lustful thoughts by thinking on them and letting them "burn" on and on within your mind. That's just making a provision for failure right there.

If you're having a problem with lust and a thought pops in your head, don't sit around and dwell on it, even if you want to. Stop yourself before you dive into the water! Talk to yourself by saying, *'I will not think about that because...'* This is where you start quoting scripture to yourself. *'My body is a living sacrifice that is holy and pleasing to God. God chose me before the creation of the world to be holy and blameless in His sight!'* (That's Romans 12:1 and Ephesians 1:4, if you're interested.)

Speak well *of* yourself *to* yourself. Don't make a provision for failure by cutting yourself down. That does no good. Build yourself up with the Word.

Make No Provision for Failure

Instead of making a provision for failure, do what the Amplified Bible version of Romans 13:14 says:

> But clothe yourself with the Lord Jesus Christ, the Messiah, and **make no provision** for [indulging] the flesh - **put a stop to thinking about the evil cravings of your physical nature** - [to gratify its] desires (lusts).

Nobody is helpless; it's just a matter of whether a person wants to control his or her thoughts – or not. Some people think that what goes on in their mind doesn't matter, but the truth is that it does matter. Continually thinking about something you know is wrong just makes you more callous to the thought. It paves the way for you to move into talking about it and then, ultimately, doing it.

Embarrass Sin Before Sin Embarrasses You!

How do you stop sin? One way is to embarrass sin before sin embarrasses you. Put your pride in check and kick the devil out of your life before he destroys you.

You don't have to hide your thoughts. If they are threatening to overwhelm you, tell somebody before you fall into sin. In fact, tell the person you're having the problem with! Explain to them why you're telling them about it. Say, "I want to embarrass sin before sin embarrasses me."

If you're having a problem with lust for other women and you're married, tell your wife. She'll take care of it or at least get you on the right road, if you'll listen to her! She may drag your rear end to the pastor or to a counselor. Let her do it. What you keep inside for pride's sake will one day make you fall. Break the power of pride over your life by deliberately coming clean about the temptation.

Now, be prepared. If you confront the person you've been lusting over, you may not get a good reaction. If you tell somebody, "I just want to apologize right now for lusting after you," they may slap you and call you a dog. They may look at you sideways and think you're nuts! But, the great thing is you'll immediately stop dwelling on the temptation!

All temptation and sin comes from either the unredeemed body or the satanic realm. Either your body is telling you what it wants or the devil is trying to tempt you with something that he hopes will steal, kill and destroy your life. Either way, you can stop temptation in its tracks if you break the power of pride over your life.

Think about it. What is the devil's biggest weakness? Pride. He likes to look good, sound good and talk good. He's slick. If you find yourself being slick too, you know where you're getting that trait from – and it ain't your Heavenly Father!

Just embarrass the devil by saying, "Get behind me, devil! I'm holy and I'm not thinking about that!" Say it out loud. Forget about other people around you for a moment. Then, go out of your way to talk about Jesus to somebody, just to irritate that idiot devil! Help someone. Do a good deed.

When you're weak, God will help you to be strong. So, draw a line in the sand with the devil. Turn the tables on him. Pretty soon, that idiot devil will start wishing that he never messed with you.

CHAPTER 12

Temptation to Slap a Hotel Clerk

Have you ever had one of those days when *nothing* goes as planned? How about the days when somebody ticks you off so bad that you want to yank your "dead man" out of his coffin…you know, just let your old flesh out long enough to slap somebody?! There have been times that I wanted to do that so bad, but I held myself back because *I* knew that *they* knew I was a Christian!

Then, there are the other times…like the day I wanted to kill a front desk clerk at a hotel in Dallas. No, I'm not proud of that day. It happened years ago, but it's still embarrassing to me and it's a great example of what happens when you aren't keen to the tapping of the Holy Spirit.

Now, most mornings, I immediately take time to pray and talk with God. I usually quote scripture to myself in the mirror and build myself up in the faith. But, on this particular day, I just didn't take the time to do it. Now, nothing serious had happened to interfere with my usual habit. I was in Dallas and scheduled to preach that night, and I'd just made plans to go jogging, swimming and sight-seeing with the pastor of the church.

When the phone rang, I was busy getting dressed and counting down the twenty-five minutes left until he was supposed to pick me up in the lobby. I felt the Lord lightly urge me to pray, but I was so busy that I thought, *I'll just pray when I get back*. I was tired and had slept longer than usual, and I needed to get ready.

Sure enough, the pastor picked me up and we went all over Dallas. We had a good time and ended up staying out longer than planned. I got back to the hotel at 5 p.m., and was scheduled to preach that night at 7 p.m.

When I got to my room, I pulled out my key card. I stuck it in the slot, but the door wouldn't open. I tried again and again, but, still, the key wouldn't work. Then, I noticed something extra hanging on the door knob…a little sign that said "Please come to the front desk." So, I went. Now, I was feeling good! My mood was great!

"Excuse me," I said to the man at the front desk, "I'm in room 216 and my card doesn't work, and there was a note that was put on the doorknob to please come to the front desk."

"Do I have a message?" I asked.

He paused, looked at me, and in a feminine voice, he said, "Well, yes. I want to let you know that your credit card has expired and we need another method of payment before we can let you back in the room."

"My credit card expired? I didn't put down my credit card," I said.

"Well," he curtly shot back, "whoever put this credit card down on this room…it's expired."

I said, "Can I look at it?"

"Sure," he said and handed me a copy of the card. It was the church's American Express and it had expired just one day. Now, for years I have paid all of my own expenses…and so, this never happens. But, this was in the early years of my ministry and back then, churches would often pay for my hotel room. In this instance, the church just didn't notice that their card was expiring on the day

I was a guest speaker.

I didn't have any identification with me because I was in a rush when I'd left my room, that I didn't even take my wallet. I had nothing on me except the room key in my pocket, so I said, "Young man, I tell you what. If you will open up the room, I will give you my credit card and you can just put the room charge on there. I'll just take care of that."

He looked at me, cocked his head and said in one long, monotone voice, "I will not open up that door unless I have another method of payment."

I thought surely he didn't understand what I'd said, so I tried to explain, "Excuse me. Listen, I even have cash. I will just pay it. All you gotta do is just open up the door. I will just pay it and we'll take care of that."

He could have cared less. In the same monotone voice, he repeated himself once again, "I will not open up the door unless we have another payment."

"No," I said, trying to talk some sense into the man, "I don't think you understand what I'm saying. I'm not trying to…it's just a mistake. They didn't realize…they didn't look at the expiration date."

"Well," he fired back in an even higher and more feminine voice, "I just tell you one thing! I will not open up that door unless I have another method of payment!"

By then, Tabasco sauce started rolling up through my veins and I was getting hot. Then, it happened. I made the transformation from "wise man of God" to "foolish vomit-licking dog" in about ten seconds flat. Had I taken a different route, this would be a different story, but no, I had to start shouting at the man.

"Now, look! Look! Look, young man! Listen to me! All you gotta do is open up the door! I will give you a credit card or I will give you cash!" I hollered. "I will pay you and we won't have this conversation anymore!"

The man shrank back and said, "You don't need to raise your voice." Then, he repeated himself again, but with even more attitude in his tone of voice than before, "I will not open up that door unless I have another method of payment."

My blood was boiling with anger and I heard a voice in my head say something that I was in full agreement with. *Hit him!* I heard it plain as day. Sure, it was a foolish voice but by then, I'd become a foolish man. This hotel had a front desk like a bank with teller windows and as I stared through the opening, I began to reason with myself thinking, *I've got enough money to get out of jail. I'm going to hit this sucker right now.*

I looked at that man, reached over the counter, grabbed him and pulled him by the shirt through the opening in the desk…I was officially losing it!

When I pulled him off of his feet, he started to squeal, "Oh no! Oh no, oh no!"

I held him a few inches from my face and through clenched teeth I said, "I'm going to beat your stinking brains out of your head!"

Then, I saw it – a phone sitting on the desk.

"You see, it says AT&T?" I asked the man as I picked up the phone and held it to his face.

"I'm going to print that on your forehead!" I yelled, "I'm going to bust you!"

Yeah, I had lost it. Here I was a preacher of the Gospel about to murder a clerk at the front desk. If I had been a woman in Jesus' parable of the wise and foolish virgins, I would have been the one without any oil and any hope! I was in trouble!

The man was squirming and whining, "Oh, no, please. Oh, no." But, I couldn't let him go. I was still shaking with anger and, then, I started talking more trash. I told him all I could think of to tell him, which was stuff like, "I'm going to break your stinking door down too! You understand? I'm going to put you in the hospital!"

That was about the time the manager came running to the man's rescue.

His voice was steady as he told me, "Sir, don't hit him, sir." I guess he figured he was dealing with a crazy man.

I was reared back and ready to bust the guy with the phone when I started sputtering my explanation to the manager, "This…stupid…wimp…fool!" I said, "I got money…in the room…and he won't open the door!"

"Whoa, control yourself, sir," he said and started trying to smooth out the situation.

"I'm…going…to bust him!" I warned.

"I'm the manager," he said, "I'll help you. What's the problem?"

I was so angry that I could barely get out the words, "The credit card…it's expired. I got money in the room…I got another card in the room. And, this fool…won't open up the…and he's wimpy and you know how he is!"

"I am so sorry sir," he said, "What's your room?"

"216!" I spat and let the man go, still fuming.

"I'll get the key and we'll go open it up right now," the manager said.

I told him, "I'll pay you!"

So, I was walking behind the manager to my room when he asked me, "What do you do for a living?"

It was a moment of truth. I didn't want to answer him. In my mind, I thought, *I work for Amway. I'm a motivational speaker.* Guilt began to replace anger, and I felt the Spirit say, *You didn't pray. You didn't put Me first. You needed Me today....*

So, instead of lying and making my own guilt worse, I came clean. "Listen," I said, "I'm a preacher."

"I can tell," he said, "I thought so."

I was shocked! I said, "Sir?"

"You're the fourth preacher that this front desk gentleman has done this to," he said. "He hates preachers. I'm going to have to fire him. I told him if he did it again, I was going to fire him."

Suddenly, I saw the situation for what it really was. The manager went on, "He saw from the credit card that it was a church. He figured you were a preacher and he just was going to harass you. I thought for a minute that I wasn't going to have to fire him...I thought we would bury him instead." It was his attempt at a joke in a sticky situation.

I said, "Sir, I'm sorry. I did wrong. God, forgive me! And I ask you to forgive me."

"Oh, that's alright," he said, "I never did like the guy."

"No, no, I'm a minister of the Gospel. I apologize. I'm sorry. I've got to apologize to him."

So, I went back down to that front desk, "Young man?" But, he didn't let me start before he started saying, "Oh, don't hit me!"

I said, "Listen. I apologize. I should not have done that. I'm a man of God."

"Yes?" he said.

I said, "I apologize...I should not have...what you did was wrong but I apologize for acting the way I did. I ask you to forgive me."

He looked at me and said, "I will NOT forgive you!" Tabasco started climbing up my legs again! So, I rebuked the thoughts of murder and said, "Shut up devil! I bind you in Jesus' name!" I apologized to the man again and went back to my room.

The pastor called me right when I walked in my room to let me know he was coming earlier than we'd planned. I told him what happened and as you'd expect, it infuriated him.

"What, you mean?! What?! You mean to tell me they wouldn't let you in the room?!"

I said, "No, listen, listen."

But he wouldn't. "I can't believe it! I'm coming down there!" He hung up the phone before I could say anything else, and it wasn't a few minutes before I was in the lobby listening to him ball out the guy. He said, "I want to tell y'all something. I put all my guest speakers in this hotel and you don't let my guest speaker in the room? It is an embarrassment to me and my church, and I'll not use any of you people anymore!" He was mad! So, do you know what I did?

I looked at him and said, "Control yourself. You need to learn to control that temper." Yeah, can you believe that? I actually told him that!

He went, "Oh, I'm sorry, Jesse."

I said, "Man what's the matter with you? Don't you know how to control yourself? Come on now. Let me pray for you." Then, I broke down and told him the story. We laughed! But do you know what the pastor said when I told him that the Lord had nudged me to pray, but I didn't?

He said, "You know what, Jesse? I had the same thing happen. I wanted to make sure you'd have a great day but I ran out and I didn't do what I normally do with the Lord."

That is a true story. Both of us neglected the inner "tapping" of the Lord that day to pray and crucify the flesh. Both of us suffered for it, and a few other people had to suffer for it too!

Your Built-In Regulator

How do you overcome a temptation like this one? The first step is to start developing your attention to the tapping of the Holy Spirit on your heart. God gave you a built-in regulator to help you along in life. Your conscience is God-created and the more time you spend in the Word and prayer, the more developed your conscience will become. It's God's way of helping you out twenty-four hours of the day.

Your emotions and your body are just followers. They're not designed to be your control-center, although many people live their whole lives governed by their own fleshly impulses.

If you have crucified the flesh and made a commitment to lean on Jesus for help that day, you'll be able to handle yourself a whole lot better when temptation comes along. If an impulse hits, you won't immediately move in that direction. Your spirit-led conscience will tap you and make you pause and think about what to do.

Your mind and body may still fight you. That's what temptation does. Your flesh may signal your mind with anger. If you're trying to overcome a vice, your flesh may try to steer you around by the nose saying, "Hey, I want this!" or "Hey, I want to do that!"

The flesh wants everything. It's like a child begging for this and that. But, it doesn't have control over what you actually do unless you *relinquish* control and agree to go with the impulses. Your mind is in control over your body, but who should be in control over your mind? Your spirit!

Crucify your flesh daily. Listen to the tapping of the Lord on your heart. If you don't, you could find yourself falling into temptation and telling an embarrassing story like this one!

CHAPTER 13

If You Say NO, Satan Will Go

Babies! They are the most powerful people in the world today. I've seen babies do the most awful things in public. They'll laugh, pass gas and vomit in the same two minutes and mama will still be there to call them sweetie. That's power, son! Babies know the power of a good scream too. Their pipes can drive a grown man to dance like a fool in the middle of a mall! They'll do just about *anything* to get what they want!

Do you know the first word that babies usually learn to express? It's "NO!" That word is short and powerful, but it gets a baby's point across quickly. Even if they can't yet speak, they will jerk their little head to the side to let you know exactly what they *don't* want from you.

You can ask a toddler, "Do you want some of this spinach?"

"No," they'll say, and they won't elaborate. They don't need to make an excuse because they don't feel guilty for saying no. If you try and force that spinach on them, they'll move their head away from your spoon and squirm to get away from you any way that they can. Buddy, you've got a battle on your hands! They're so fast that you'll miss their mouth and hit their cheek with the spoon. *Whap*! The spinach is going to the floor. As an adult, you may like to think you're the most powerful one in the room, but that baby is controlling the situation!

If, by some miracle of God, you manage to shovel a spoonful in their mouth, it's going to come right back at you if they don't want it. Babies will spit strained carrots in your face and not think anymore about it. They don't care. They've figured out early on in life that they've got free will, a God-given right to say "no!"

You Have a Right to Say "NO!"

Temptation may come and the devil may try and shovel sin down your throat. But, if you know that it's going to leave a bad taste in your mouth, you have every right *not* to swallow his lies. Just do what babies do. Jerk your head to the side, say "NO!" and let the sin fall to the floor.

Like babies, you have free will and when you choose to say "no," you don't have to feel like you've got to elaborate. Remember that when Jesus was tempted in the wilderness, He didn't make excuses. He didn't say, "You know, devil, I would fall down and worship you, but I just don't feel like it today." Jesus simply said, *"It is written..."* which basically meant 'NO. It's wrong and I'm not doing it. I'm doing what God says no matter what you tempt me with.'

Stand strong in your convictions and *keep* resisting. Don't let impulses or the deceptive measures of the devil get to you. It won't be long before he flees, just like he fled when Jesus resisted him in the wilderness. You've got to understand that the devil is impatient. He's only going to stick around for just so long, and, then, he's out of there. Remind yourself of that when you're in the enduring time.

Hot Tomato! Whoa, Baby!?

Years ago, I remember meeting a woman at church who had the most beautiful baby girl. The baby was wearing, what looked to me, a baptismal gown. It was long, white and just gorgeous. When the woman asked me if I wanted to hold her baby, I said, "I'd love to." What a precious gift of God.

Well, the blessing stopped right there. As I told the mother, "This is a beautiful child," the baby started contorting and her pretty little face began to turn red. In about three seconds flat, she looked like a tomato in a wedding gown. The girl was struggling! I could hear her straining, and, suddenly, I got a revelation.

"Oh, my God, what are we gonna do here!" I said. Then, the smell hit me. Now, the kid was wearing a diaper, thank God, but it only muffled the noises and sure didn't help the mother's pride. Inside, I felt like hollering, "Ughhhhh!" I didn't. I endured.

"I'm *so* sorry," she said as she turned to the baby with a horrified look on her face and pleaded, "Stop, honey...stop." That baby wasn't about to stop. She could have cared less that she was in the arms of the most righteous Reverend Jesse Duplantis. She just babbled at her mother and just kept doing what had to be done *until* she was done.

It was only by the grace of Almighty God that I was able to resist the urge to say, "Good God Almighty! This baby stinks! I think she's rotting out my suit! Somebody take her!" But, I didn't do that. Instead, I stayed right where I was and kept a smile on my face, and, in due time, I was able to gracefully give her back to her mother as if it hadn't bothered me at all. When the baby passed out of my arms, thank God, the smell went with her. Suddenly, I was free and it felt great!

That's how you have to be when it comes to temptation. You have to keep on resisting the urge to give into your fleshly impulses. Don't give a halfhearted "no" to temptation. If you do, your flesh is going to bowl you over.

Resisting temptation isn't easy, but the Bible says that God will never allow you to have more than you can endure. 1 Corinthians 10:13 says, *"...but God is faithful, who will not suffer you to be tempted above that ye are able; but will with the temptation also make a way to escape, that ye may be able to bear it."*

That baby didn't care at all because she was just doing what needed to be done. Resisting is what needs to be done in your life so that you don't end up living a hellish life here on earth – one that is filled with more problems and backtracking than is necessary. Why put yourself through more Hell on earth than you need to?

When you make a choice to resist temptation, you're not going to feel altogether comfortable. Like that baby, you may squirm and turn red in the face while you're experiencing the pressure of temptation. That's what enduring is about. Just keep doing what needs to be done – keep resisting! Don't let what others think about you get in the way. It's what God thinks that really matters. Hold out and it won't be long before temptation will cease and you'll be able to thank God for helping you make it through the situation with grace.

Resist, Believe God and Laugh at Anxiety

You weren't created to be defeated. It may be tempting, but you don't have to *accept* defeat. You don't have to live like most

Christians. You can make the *decision* to resist the devil. Too many people want healing, peace and joy to just happen, but you have to pull on the work of the cross. You do that by making a decision to believe God and speak the Word in faith. It's tempting to be lazy with the things of God, but that kind of thinking is the quickest path to defeat. Faith works, but it only works if you apply it.

Anxiety is so common today because we are living in a fast-paced world. Sickness steals more time, energy and money from people than almost anything else. These things aren't God's best. To live in anxiety is hellish! To live sick, sad and disgusted is hellish! Who wants that? No one! So, why do so many Christians put up with it?

You don't have to put up with being sick, sad, anxious or disgusted. I don't care if everybody around you is living with a box of tissue under their arm to take care of the green stuff and popping pills to handle their anxiety, you don't have to do it. There is a better way for you. Get in God's presence and learn how to release worry if that's your issue. Read the Word and learn to trust in the Lord and not fear. Fear is at the root of a lot of problems, but the Word says that *"There is no fear in love; but perfect love casteth out fear: because fear hath torment. He that feareth is not made perfect in love"* (1 John 4:18).

Anxiety is torment. Is torment going to be part of Heaven? No! It's part of Hell. So, if you're putting up with it, you're agreeing to have a little Hell right here on earth. Why do that? God has made a way of escape for you.

Don't let the lure of a quick fix deter you from going to God and getting at the root of the problem. Remember that the love of God is what can banish that problem from your life. *"We love Him, because He first loved us"* (1 John 4:19). God's love is in you and it's what can help you find real peace and security so that all those fear-based issues can just fall away.

Emotions Can't Be Trusted

Emotions can change from one minute to the next, so you can't trust them. That's why the Bible tells us we are to live from faith to faith. *"For therein is the righteousness of God revealed from faith to faith: as it is written, The just shall live by faith"* (Romans 1:17). Emotions are usually governed by something you see, feel, smell, taste or touch – and our senses pick up different things from moment to moment. But, the Word of God never changes.

Some people think that every emotion they feel needs to be drawn out to the tenth degree. That's what I call Hell on earth, because the devil will try and play with your emotions. He's the one who whispers, "It's not working, go ahead and do whatever you want. It doesn't matter." If you listen to his lies, you'll make bad decisions in your life and end up living much lower than you should. You may end up feeling like you really are living in Hell right here on earth.

You can change your own emotions. If you feel down, you can feel a lot better simply by praying, spending quiet time with God or meditating on the Word. Whatever negative emotion you release to Him is one less thing you have to carry around with you all day. If you're sad, you don't have to let yourself sink all the way down.

Stop your mind before it wanders off and starts just rehearsing all the things you don't like about yourself or your life. That's torment, and remember where it comes from. It's not from God, and so it's not for you. Instead, make a decision to say, "No. I will not think on those things." Then, remind yourself of the scripture.

> *Finally, brethren, whatsoever things are true, whatsoever things are honest, whatsoever things are just, whatsoever things are pure, whatsoever things are lovely, whatsoever things are of good report; if there be any virtue, and if there be any praise, think on these things.*
>
> *Those things, which ye have both learned, and received, and heard, and seen in me, **do**: and the God of **peace** shall be with you.*
>
> Philippians 4:8-9

When you say "no" to those negative thoughts and replace them with what God has said, you are stopping deception before it can defeat you. You are opening your eyes to what is good and turning a deaf ear to the lies of the devil. That's active resistance. It's what I do and it works.

You see, it's what I choose to do that is going to make the difference in my life. Nobody can believe the Word for me. I've got to believe it for myself. *I* determine whether I am going to let problems overtake me or stand firm on the Word.

When the devil comes at me like a flood, I choose to turn the tables on him. He thinks he's going to hurt me by attacking me. Instead, I just get into prayer and release the worry to God. Then, I laugh at the devil's plans for my defeat because I know that I will prevail.

I'd Rather Laugh Than Cry

I've decided that I'd rather laugh than cry. I tried sad, and I didn't like it! To me, bawling and squawking doesn't change anything. It may be an emotional release, but it sure doesn't bring me any closer to victory. What changes the circumstances in my life and brings me closer to victory is when I choose to see what God says about my situation. Then, I make light of what the devil is trying to do to me. I let God's Word become final authority, and that's what helps me to laugh at the devil's attempts to hurt me.

When I look at my background, my family and the area of the world where I grew up, I think, *God, how could you ever use somebody like me?* But, He did, and He is continuing to use me, in spite of how I think, where I grew up and how I learned to deal with life as a kid. Why? Because I have chosen to believe Him, to walk with Him and to say "no" to the lies of the devil that would have had me believe that I was without hope. Nobody is without hope!

I have chosen to accept His joy because I need it to give me strength. Why would I want to want to focus on every negative aspect of life? What does that do but bring me down? I want to focus on what God has done and what I can have through my faith in His Word because it lifts me up.

God has done more in my life than I could have ever done on my own. The devil fights me and I have to resist temptation like everyone else, but I know that if I stick with God and have faith in His Word, I'm going to overcome. I'm going to come out smelling like a rose and doing more than I ever thought I could do.

I've made a decision that I'm not going to let the devil change my destiny. What he does and says makes no difference to me. I shut him down! Even though he tries to convince me that I'll never make it, I refuse to agree with him. He's a fool, rejected and on his way to a fiery lake. I'm a child of God who has the mind of Christ; I'm accepted and on my way to a Heavenly home. The devil and I are not going to the same place after judgment! So, why do I have to go his way while I'm living here on earth? I don't and neither do you.

The devil may try to kill, steal from you and destroy God's plans for your life. Resist his efforts and speak the Word knowing that you will *live, prosper* and see God's *best* come to pass in your life. When you develop this mind-set of faith in God, you are saying "no" to destruction and "yes" to abundance.

The Power of the Holy Ghost

The only way to say "no" to the devil is to say "yes" to the Holy Ghost. The Bible says that Jesus was "full of the Holy Ghost." That's why He could say no to the devil. That's how He could live His life, knowing that He was destined for a cruel cross.

Luke 4:1-2 says, *"And Jesus being full of the Holy Ghost returned from Jordan, and was led by the Spirit into the wilderness, Being forty days tempted of the devil..."* It took the fullness of the Holy Ghost to get Jesus through temptation. How much more then do you need to have the fullness of the Holy Ghost working in your life? If Jesus needed it to combat temptation, you are going to need it to combat temptation.

There is power in the Holy Ghost. He is the very presence of God, empowering His children with all strength and boldness to resist and defeat the devil. That's why I believe that when people say the Holy Ghost isn't for today or that you cannot approach God boldly, they are missing it by a hundred miles. Their intellectual ability is getting in the way of them seeing Jesus for Who He is – our pathway to Almighty God. (See John 14:6)

When you go boldly to the throne of grace, just as you are, and you say, "God, give me everything You have for me." He will give you His Holy Spirit, and within that Holy Spirit are the nine gifts and nine fruits of the Holy Spirit – the fullness of the Godhead bodily.

Hebrews 4:15-16 tells us, *"For we have not an high priest which cannot be touched with the feeling of our infirmities; but was in all points tempted like as we are, yet without sin. Let us therefore come boldly unto the throne of grace, that we may obtain mercy, and find grace to help in time of need."*

The Bible reassures us of our position with God when it says, *"...because as He is, so are we in this world"* (1 John 4:17). Our love is made perfect in Him! We can be bold!

I'm tired of people saying that we aren't what the Word says we are. We are more than conquerors. If God be for us, who can be against us? I've decided to stand on God's Word, glory to God, and learn to say "no" to the devil.

When temptation comes your way, all you have to do is say "no." Refuse depression. Refuse drugs. Refuse alcohol. Refuse lust and every diabolical thing that comes from the pit. You can do it because you have power over your own flesh. You have the God-given right to choose what you will do and who you will serve.

"And if it seem evil unto you to serve the LORD, choose you this day whom ye will serve..." (Joshua 24:15). Do you want to live for God or your flesh? Notice that the Word commands you to choose this day whom you will serve. What are you going to do today? Serving God is something you do.

You can say you love God, but it's what you do that shows your heart. Jesus said, *"If ye love Me, keep My commandments"* (John 14:15). In other words, 'Show Me. Live right.' God could have just told us that He loved us but He took it a step further. He showed us His great love by giving us His Son, Jesus. That's love in action. That's the power of our God.

When you say "yes" to His Holy Ghost and accept the fullness of Him, then you're able to be bold. Remember, the disciples were a bunch of wishy-washy men before the day of Pentecost. After the Holy Ghost came down, they were filled with more than just the ability to speak in other languages and spread the Gospel. They were filled with boldness to do what God wanted them to do.

You have something God wants you to do, a destiny that is good in His sight. The devil will try and fight you tooth and nail along the way. Along the way, the devil will do his best to tempt you to go the wrong way and to deceive you with all sorts of lies. But the Holy Ghost will give you the boldness you need to say "Get out of here, devil!" and continue living right.

The Holy Ghost is also called the Comforter. In John 14:26, Jesus said, *"But the Comforter, which is the Holy Ghost, whom the Father will send in My name, He shall teach you all things, and bring all things to your remembrance, whatsoever I have said unto you."* It's comforting to know that the Holy Ghost will teach you and bring the Word to your memory. There are times when the devil may fight you and a scripture will just come right up in your mind – that's the Holy Ghost at work, reminding you to use the Word as a spiritual weapon against deception.

The devil is a liar and his way of thinking is always at odds with God's Word. But when you know the Word and you have the Holy Ghost operating in your life, you can recognize his deceiving tactics and say "no" when he tries to twist the Word to suit the flesh. You can expose his lie, avoid his trap and live free.

Lose Yourself in God

People ask me why I speak in tongues in public. I can't help myself. Sometimes, I lose myself in God. I might be at a restaurant in a buffet line and just start praying out loud. I'm not embarrassed to be a Christian. Before I was saved, I cussed in public. So, now that I know God, why can't I pray in public?

People talk about their lustful activities in public. Why can't I talk about my God in public? I'm not trying to get in anybody's business, but I don't want to hide who I am just because of what others might think. I'm beyond that. I know who I am and Whose I am.

I don't care if other people don't believe me; it's what I believe that matters because that is what is going to affect my future. You see, you have to get to a place where the opinions of the world don't matter so much. Sure, you want people to like you, but, sometimes, they just won't.

Falling into the world's sinful lifestyle won't make you any more liked or accepted by people. It won't fulfill the void of wanting to be wanted, loved, and admired or anything like that. Only God can fulfill that need you have. I've learned that in my life and so, I'm not living for other people. I care about people, because everyone matters, but I don't let what *they* think about me determine what I think about myself.

The more you dive into your relationship with God, the more you "lose yourself" in Him, and the more you will actually find out who you are and what you need in life. Before that, you're just living according to what other people have told you that you should have, need and want. God can blow all those preconceived ideas out of the water. He will help you to zone in on truth and get rid of all those human ideas of what is going to make you happy. God will give you more knowledge and wisdom about yourself than you could ever conjure up on your own.

Some people think I'm arrogant, but I'm just intensely saved. I'm filled with the glory of divine righteousness. I don't struggle with identity issues and I'm not wishy-washy. Why? Because I'm full of the Holy Ghost and I am free! So, when I speak the Word, I believe it! I don't water it down. I see blessings come my way, and I don't mind praising God about them. I see His miracle of provision and I shout! I see His healing power flowing and I get excited. It doesn't make a lick of difference if people like me or not or if they believe me or not. It makes every difference if they know Jesus and believe Him for themselves.

Your spiritual activity will reach its greatest intensity when you are so filled with the glory of His divine righteousness, love and power that you are only conscious of God. When all thought of yourself is stripped away and you are able to concentrate only on Him and on what He would have you to do for others...that's when you know you're at the peak!

Don't spend your whole life thinking about yourself, your problems, your temptations and your weaknesses. It's time to get beyond yourself, and it starts when you get full of the Holy Ghost. There is a time to focus on you, but it is a much better life when you are focused on others. Ask yourself, "Am I so full of the Spirit of God that I'm not thinking about myself anymore? Am I conscious of God right now? Am I conscious of Him living in me and working through me right now?"

When you are living like that, you don't get offended nearly as easily. You don't care if people curse you, because you see through it to the root issue. They need God. You don't care if somebody else isn't walking in love because you have enough love for the both of you. You don't care what the devil tries to show you; you are quick to resist him and say, "no." When you're living like that, you are in touch with more of God than most people ever even get a glimpse of. You have lost yourself in Him. You are walking in His divine love and because of that, you're also walking in His divine power.

Criticism Often Comes from the Religious Crowd

When you make a stand for God and start being bold in your faith, get ready for criticism. I find that the people who don't want to see you succeed are often the religious crowd! They want you to be sick and always believing. They want you to fall into temptation, so they don't feel so bad about living in the flesh all week long.

People don't always want the best for you and the devil will use people you never thought he'd use to try and squelch your boldness for God. Don't listen to the criticism. In Jesus' day, the fiercest criticism came out of the mouths of the Pharisees and the Sadducees. They criticized the fact that Jesus healed people on the Sabbath. They didn't like it that He spoke truth with boldness. They wanted Him to speak and act without conviction or boldness like they did!

Religious people are like weeds in a beautiful garden. They choke out the life! Jesus didn't mix words when they criticized Him. *"...Jesus answered, Ye neither know Me, nor my Father: if ye had known Me, ye should have known My Father also"* (John 8:19). He didn't care if He was talking to the religious crowd. Jesus made certain that no one choked the life out of Him.

Don't be easily discouraged by what people say. If you're past having doubts, then don't let someone else convince you to accept their doubt. Don't let them steal your confidence away. If you've gotten a revelation about deception and somebody tries to tell you not to be so bold about it, let their words roll off of you like water on a duck's back. They don't know what they're saying. You are the one whose eyes have been opened to the devil's tactics. You are the one who is going to succeed. Don't let some unbelieving Christian talk you out of God's best.

Guard Your Neck, Old Man!

Have you ever watched an old vampire movie? Have you ever noticed how much vampires like necks? They start there, and before you know it, the innocent person is sucked dry of every drop of life. The devil is the same way. He's looking for a soft spot to bite – some weak area in your life. He wants to bite there first and, then, suck the life right out of you. Don't let him do it! Guard your neck!

You know, most sin seems to start at the neck. If you ask someone, "How did you get that big bruise on your neck there, boy?" They won't come clean about it. They'll say, "Oh, I was playing golf and the guy swung and the club fell out and hit me right in the neck" or "I was trying to get in my car and slammed my neck." Lying dog! Somebody sucked your neck, that's what happened! Sin starts at the neck. It doesn't make a difference if you're a hormone-raging teenager or a sixty-year-old man – temptation is temptation.

I know some of you teenagers think, "Ah, those old people don't do that." Yes, they do! Sin has no age bracket. Lust doesn't stop working at a certain age. Given the option, an old man will fall into sin just as easy as a young man; there are just less old woman saying "yes." Don't let that shock you. It's the truth! Women just have more sense than men when it comes to that area of life.

One night, a 76-year-old man woke me up by banging on my hotel room door just to tell me, "Pray, I need a woman!" I thought that at seventy-six that mess was over with, but apparently not. I said, "What's the matter with you?" He looked at me desperately and said, "I ain't dead! I need a woman!"

I had to pray for the old man and get rid of the spirit of lust! I talked to him for a while about it, and when he left my room, I started thinking, "Seventy-six? What's the matter? What does he eat!?" The pastor told me later, "If you can help him, help him. He's driving me crazy!"

Let Me Out, Old Woman!

Another time, I met a 73-year-old woman after a crusade who had the same problem. I was just walking off the platform and, suddenly, this sweet looking old lady ran towards me, hit me and pushed me in a closet by the stage. I was in shock! She shut that door and immediately said, "I need a man!"

"Open that door right now!" I said to her.

She said, "I believe you're a man of God. I need prayer! I want a man now!"

I said, "You open that door!" I didn't want to knock her out of the way because she was 73 years old, and I could just read the headlines – "Evangelist Found in Closet with 73-year-old woman." I had to get out.

She wouldn't stop until I prayed, but she kept saying, "I believe you hear God. Pray for me! I want a husband!" So, I prayed.

"God," I said, "Give this lady a husband, quickly!"

Immediately, the old woman opened the door and I walked out. "Thank you!" she said and left. I was blown away.

Well, six months passed and I was preaching at the Shreveport Civic Center when she walked up to me…with a man on her arm. "It works!" she said. "I want you to meet my husband."

The man said, "You prayed for my wife, for me, didn't you?"

"Yeah," I said, "I tell you what, it kind of shocked me. She's seventy-three."

He said, "I tell you what. She shocks me too."

I asked, "You need prayer?"

"Definitely!" he said.

The Ability to Command Is In Your Spirit

You can say what Jesus said: *"Get thee hence, Satan: for it is written..."* (Matt. 4:10). You can speak whatever God said in His Word as a command. The ability is in your spirit. You can say, "Get thee hence, Satan! I will resist and you will flee! There is no weapon formed against me that is going to prosper! By His stripes I was healed! I walk in love and God's perfect love casts out all fear! I am overcoming the world because of what Jesus did. I'm living by faith in the Son of God, who loved me and died for me!"

God has made you a commander, not a janitor. You don't walk around cleaning up your own mess. You go to God and let His blood wash you clean so that you can command the devil to flee – and do it with confidence. With confidence, you denounce sin. With confidence, you surrender yourself to God's way of doing things. The ability to command the devil to get under your feet is in your spirit.

You can take anything that comes your way, and command it to go, but if you don't use your ability to command, the devil will defeat you. You have to speak with authority. Using your authority with confidence works with the devil, and it also works with people in business.

Before I do business, I pray. Before I buy a car, I pray. I ask God for wisdom, I do my own research, and, then, I speak with confidence and authority. I don't allow any fear to show. What am I doing? I'm using my God-given ability to command the situation. It's not my will but God's will that needs to be done. So, I deny myself, surrender to God and speak with authority.

I was talking to a business man once about a $5.9 million dollar deal and I used the ability to command. He started telling me what he couldn't do, and I started saying what we would do.

"Well, we can't do this," he said,

"This is what we're going to do," I told him. "You listen to me because God has said it!" He wasn't saved, but he just agreed with me. I spoke with authority because I had the mind of Christ about the situation. I'd already prayed and I wasn't insecure about the situation. So, I didn't use unsure words like "we'll try" or "maybe this will work."

Commands are direct statements. This is what I *will* do. This is what *is* going to happen. I didn't make wishy-washy statements because God never told me to be a "trier" – He told me to be a doer. It works with the Word, and it works with the world.

When you use the ability you have to command the devil to flee, you aren't in wishy-washy mode. You aren't "trying." You are doing. If you just try to rebuke or resist the devil halfheartedly, you'll lose.

If you base your commands on some personal philosophy, commanding won't work. It'll just be a lot of hot air. But, if you base your commands on the Word of God, then you've got something backing you. The devil is going to run from you because you're using God's Word. Satan has no other choice but to recede when he's confronted with God Almighty's Word.

Don't play games. If you don't kick the devil out of your mind, he'll take over. If you don't kick him out of your house, he'll try to kill all the joy and peace for miles around! Being saved alone doesn't make for a great life; it just makes for a great afterlife. It's what you do with the information God gives you in His Word that is going to make for a great life.

The devil will try and make your life hellish, even if you're saved, full of the Holy Ghost and on your way to Heaven. Turn the tables on him. Learn to say "no" to the lies he would try and fool you with.

When he comes with sin, say "no" and stand on the Word. When he comes with sadness, say "no" and go to God for joy. When he says that he's going to take your job, say "no" and stand on God's Word for favor and provision. Don't live below your destiny. God wants you to live His way, the best way, and enjoy an abundant, heavenly life.

"The thief cometh not, but for to steal, and to kill, and to destroy: I am come that they might have life, and that they might have it more abundantly" (John 10:10).

Say "NO" to Pharisee Ways

Too many Christians walk around saying how much God is doing for them, but they can't keep themselves out of hideous sin. Jesus called religious people who did that hypocrites.

Today, when I see a preacher talking about all the revelation God is giving him, and then I find out he's living in deep sin, I want to holler, "Why don't you quit stomping the blood of Jesus Christ!? I'll tell you what God's given you. He's given you some wisdom that you haven't used."

Do you know what Jesus was looking for when He was on the earth? Faith! Not perfection, but faith. He was looking for somebody who wasn't a hypocrite like the Pharisees and Sadducees; somebody who would let Him show Himself strong in.

I believe that Jesus isn't looking for people who are interested in building their own kingdom but for those who are willing to die to self and build His kingdom. He's looking for more men and women like Paul the Apostle who are willing to die to their own desires and say, *"It's not me that liveth, but Christ that liveth in me."* That's what Jesus is looking for. He's looking for somebody who is willing to not just say what He says but to do anything He asks.

The world needs to see believers like you and me not just talking about Jesus but acting like Him – strong, loving, direct and obeying the Father everyday, and not just on Sundays. It's not about being some holy-rolling person who isn't in touch with the realities of life. It's about letting God's nature win over your own weakness. It's about being strong and living your convictions so that your very life brings glory to God.

You can deal with any Temptation that is common to man

Sexual Temptation

The Word of GOD

Personal Convictions

CHAPTER 14

"Forni-what!?"
Dealing with Sexual Temptations
That are "Common to Man"

There are many ways that the devil tempts people, and he often uses sex. In this chapter, I'm going to share some of the sexual temptations that are common to man. The Bible says that there are common temptations, but God is faithful. He'll never allow you to be tempted with anything that you aren't able to overcome. He says that He will *"also make a way to escape, that ye may be able to bear it."* (1 Corinthians 10:13).

"Forni-what?"

The Bible isn't an outdated book. It may be old, but Jesus doesn't change and the Word is our manual for living clean in a dirty world. I like to say it's a welfare book. It's there for your welfare, and if you obey it, you'll fare well!

Although there are many scriptures about sex outside of the marriage covenant, here is one that I've chosen to include in this teaching:

> *Mortify therefore your members which are upon the
> earth; fornication, uncleanness, inordinate affection,
> evil concupiscence, and covetousness, which is idolatry.*

*For which things' sake the wrath of God cometh on
the children of disobedience.*

Colossians 3:5-6

The word "fornication" is used to describe a sexual relationship
outside the bonds of a covenant that we call marriage. The technical
distinction between fornication and adultery is that adultery involves
married persons while fornication involves those who are unmarried.
The New Testament often uses the word fornication in a general
sense for any unchaste sexual behavior between two people.

A lot of people think that God is just trying to tell you not to
have sex outside the covenant because he wants to keep something
from you. That's just not true. God wants to protect you from being
used by people who don't care enough about you to commit to you.

God loves you and wants to help you with this, but before you
can say "no," you have to realize that it's not OK in God's eyes to
link your body with anybody who comes along. Although many
people think that it's outdated, the Bible is pretty clear on this.

Of the list of sins found in the writings of the Apostle Paul, the
word fornication is found in five of them and is first on the list each
time (1 Corinthians 5:11; Colossians 3:5). In the Book of
Revelation, fornication is symbolic of how idolatry and pagan
religion defiles true worship of God (Revelation 14:8; 17:4). So,
regardless of our current society's "no rules" way of living, I'd say
God was against it – wouldn't you?

When A Man Is Hungry, He Eats – Right?

In biblical times, many people used the excuse that when a man is hungry he must eat and when he has sexual desire he must fulfill it – in any way he can. But, this was man's reasoning, not God's will. This was the reasoning that man had to follow every impulse. It's just not true. God ordained certain purposes for the body according to 1 Corinthians 6:13.

In the Bible, God tells us that the digestive functions of the stomach and sexual functions of the body are not one in the same. Food is only temporary. Sexuality, on the other hand, reaches our innermost being because it is through sex that the mystery of two becoming one occurs (Ephesians 5:31-32). It is a function of the body that is "for the Lord," which means it's dedicated not only to your pleasure but also to His purposes.

The Bible calls sexual immorality a sin against the body. In other words, God created the body to work within certain guidelines and when we cause our bodies to stray from those guidelines, the body will experience the repercussions. Many say that when the privilege of sexual relations is abused through fornication or adultery, what God meant for blessing becomes a cause for judgment. I'm not sure about that, but I do know this – God said to keep sex within the boundaries of the covenant of marriage, and He knows what He's talking about! After all, He made us.

The scripture goes on to say, *"Or do you not know that your body is the temple of the Holy Spirit who is in you, whom you have from God, and you are not your own. For you were bought with a price; therefore glorify God in your body and in your spirit, which are God's"* (1 Corinthians 6:19-20, NASB).

You are a temple – a sanctuary for God to dwell in! If you're saved, then the Holy Spirit of God resides within you. Just a few verses before this verse in 1 Corinthians, it says that when we link ourselves to another person in immorality, we literally link Jesus Christ to them! Oh, man, just think about that for a minute!

Avoiding the Temptation

If you're not saved, you may have a difficult time resisting the temptation to have sex with whoever says "yes" to you. It's normal. The body is made to procreate and so it wants to do its thing! But, God wants to help you put your spirit first.

If your mind isn't renewed to the Word, your will is weakened. Thus, you'll need all the help you can get from God in avoiding sex outside of marriage. But, if you are born again, I believe that abstaining is a lot more possible for you. It might be tough, but it's a temptation you can resist.

You're not an animal. You're a speaking spirit and you have God inside of you to help you out. He is your "cold shower." He's not going to scream "Stop!" in your ear when you're in a compromising position, but He will be faithful to nudge your heart and let you know you're going too far. You'll do best if you don't put yourself in precarious situations, because it's a whole lot easier to resist before you're into it hot and heavy.

Use the tips I shared with you in the chapter on the mind and the mouth. Let your mouth speak the Word and that'll stop a situation from going too far – quick! It's amazing what the name of Jesus will do in a sexually heated situation! Speak in tongues. Man, that'll stop it from going too far – nothing like a little tongue talking session to shut down the flesh!

Don't Be Condemned! God Is Good!

God is a good Father and He loves you. He's not trying to keep something good from you. He just wants the best for you – and His best is a committed marriage relationship. He doesn't want to see you used or abused. You're more than just a body and God wants you to have a relationship with a person who recognizes that. He wants you to have somebody who loves you enough to commit to you and say, "No matter what happens, I love you and I'm with you! I DO!"

But, if you're single and you've lost your way in this area, Jesus doesn't want you to feel condemnation today. He does, however, want you to be convicted of your sin and realize that it's not good to go on living this way. (You may want to read 1 John chapter one.)

You see, God meant for sex to be a wonderful thing. It is His gift to husband and wife – a way to celebrate the passion and joy of being together and perpetuate the cycle of life. But, if you've found that you've strayed from God's original plan and have slipped into sin in this area, all hope is not lost! God created The Way, The Truth and The Life through Jesus' shed blood on the cross for you to be cleansed of all sin – and He'll give you the strength to resist further sin.

Sexual sin washes out in the blood just as easily as any other sin. When Jesus washes your sins away, He washes them away for good. They're gone from His memory and He never holds it against you again. If you want Him to know about it, you'll have to bring it up because He forgot it the minute you said, "Forgive me, Jesus." Once you say that, it's like you never did it in the first place.

Single and Entangled In a Sexual Relationship

If you're entangled in a sexual relationship and you're not married, God will give you the strength to end the sexual part of your relationship (or make the decision to get married) and resist the temptation to sin any further.

However, if you decide to marry, consider what the Word of God says in 2 Corinthians 6:14-15 (NIV), *"Do not be yoked together with unbelievers. For what do righteousness and wickedness have in common? Or what fellowship can light have with darkness? What harmony is there between Christ and Belial? What does a believer have in common with an unbeliever?"*

It is important that both of you know God and want to make changes in your lives. It's not easy, I know. These kinds of situations are filled with complex issues and feelings. That is just what sin does to a life. It complicates it. But, life in God is simple – it's always that "right thing to do" that seems so hard and, yet, is so clear-cut.

Do Not Be Deceived

Remember, no matter what the situation, having an intimate relationship outside of marriage is not God's plan. And unless a person repents from the sin of fornication, the scriptures say in 1 Corinthians 6:9-10 that they will not enter the Kingdom of Heaven.

The Bible warns us not to be deceived. Integrity and morality must be traits of a Christian if they expect to see Heaven. This means that even though sex outside of marriage may be common today, it is still a sin in God's eyes and it will keep a lot of people out of Heaven if they don't repent and give their lives back to God. Don't let this happen to you.

God will forgive you of all sin and restore you. He can do it if you'll let Him. Will you open your life to His grace today? If so, all you have to do is admit that you are in sin and let God know you need His forgiveness of the sin. Then, repent. Make a quality decision to turn away from sin today. You can do it! God is ready and willing to forgive and help you. Reach out to Him.

If You're In, Get Out!

When two people commit to one another in the covenant of marriage, God seals the union and blesses it. He doesn't want you going outside the union for sexual gratification. Adding anybody else's flesh to your "one flesh" marriage isn't God's best. So, if you're "in" additional sexual relationships, let me help you: GET OUT!

Man, getting into a sexual relationship with a person other than your spouse is bad news – spiritually, physically and, eventually, it costs you financially too. Divorce is one of the most expensive decisions you can make. And, according to the people I've counseled and heard from, you haven't heard about Hell until you've been through a divorce! It's like being thrown into the lake of fire early!

The covenant of marriage is an extremely strong union and, according to God, it is unbreakable in the realm of the spirit. God sees the married couple as one, even going so far as to tell us that when both husband and wife are not in agreement, their very prayers are hindered. So, it stands to reason that it is not God's will that you have relations with anyone other than your spouse.

In Exodus 20, God outlined some commandments for the children of Israel. One of them was *Thou Shalt Not Commit Adultery* as recorded in verse fourteen. The reason for God doing this was simple – to keep the foundation of society (marriage) intact.

God knew that it would be devastating to one spouse if the other broke his/her marital promise and strayed. You see, God knows the heart of a man. He knows the heart of a woman. After all, He created them! Together, husband and wife are one in His sight, and His best is that they remain faithful through good times and bad.

It's About Trust

There are so many reasons why God is so clear cut about this. One is because of trust. Trust is essential to any good marriage. If you don't have it, you're missing a major piece of the marriage covenant.

When a spouse has casual sex or develops an intimate sexual relationship outside the marriage, the mutual trust between the married couple is completely destroyed. Not only is their relationship cruelly undermined, but the children receive a confused message about love, trust and fidelity between husbands and wives.

Kids learn how to live life through the parent's example. An adulterous spouse teaches a kid that it is OK to break promises and hurt others – as long as it makes you happy. It can start a family pattern and that's not what God wants for His children. It's just not God's will for any husband or wife to destroy trust and hurt their spouse and children through adultery.

It's Not Your Body to Give Away to Someone Else

Let the husband render to his wife the affection due
her, and likewise also the wife to her husband. The wife
does not have authority over her own body, but the
husband does.

And likewise, the husband does not have authority
over his own body but the wife does.

1 Corinthians 7:3-4, NKJV

This means that, according to God, if you're married you don't have the right to give your body to anyone else. Sexually, it is your gift to your spouse and you shouldn't be passing that gift on to anybody else! There is no gray area here! Affection is not a one-sided thing. It is your duty in marriage to show love in action. In 1 Corinthians 6:13, it tells us that God ordained certain purposes for the body. *"But whoso committeth adultery with a woman lacketh understanding: he that doeth it destroyeth his own soul"* (Proverbs 6:32).

You see, although it might not feel like it, adultery is actually a form of sexual immorality. And, like fornication, the Bible calls sexual immorality a sin against the body. Like I just mentioned, God created the body to work within certain guidelines and when we cause our bodies to stray from those guidelines, the body will experience the repercussions. Those repercussions are usually on a mental or emotional level, but they might be on a physical level too.

If you're struggling with another relationship, know that God's will is for you to make a clean break from it. The best thing to do is to first, repent. Ask for God's forgiveness and end that relationship. I know it might be difficult because you've established emotional ties, but that person isn't worth going to Hell over!

No matter how crummy your marriage is now, God can restore it and make it better than it ever was before. God is waiting with open arms to forgive you and to restore your marriage. He can do it if you want Him to and if you are both willing to allow Him to.

The Lord is with you when times are easy, and He's with you when times are tough. Your pastor can counsel and help you to rebuild the marriage relationship, but, remember, marriage tips alone won't cut it. It's putting God first place that saves us from the situations we put ourselves into. Thankfully, He's always there – arms wide open and ready to heal whatever hurts are in your life.

Sexual Confusion

If you're struggling with sexual confusion, let me tell you something, God didn't make a mistake when He made you. The devil is just trying to cause confusion in your life by warping your opinion of your sexuality. He may have been trying to chip away at your identity since you were little – but that doesn't mean he has to win. The devil is a liar and an idiot, but he's slick and will use anything he can to try and destroy God's creation.

God planned your sexuality. He planned where you would be born and the time of your birth, etc. In fact, you are so special to Him that He gave you fingerprints that no one else will ever have. He made you to be just who you are, His prized possession! Ephesians 2:10 (NASB) says, *"For we are His workmanship, created in Christ Jesus for good works, which God prepared beforehand that we should walk in them."*

Nothing the devil does to try and steal, kill or destroy is irreversible – including sexuality. If you're a woman, God made you to desire a man. If you're a man, He made you to desire a woman. If you don't, then there is some confusion going on in your mind and body, and God is the only one who can help you undo what's happened in your life. God loves you and wants to untangle your mind, your emotions and your desires.

Remember, just because a person is on one path in life doesn't mean they can't change, turn around and go another way. God can peel off any label society puts on. I've heard people say, "Brother Jesse, I fell in love and I just can't help it if that person is the same sex as me."

I don't doubt that a person can fall in love with someone of the same sex. Personally, I wouldn't have a problem with homosexuality at all. I could care less what somebody does, but the Word speaks against it in Romans 1:24-32; 1 Corinthians 6:9; Jude 1:7 – and I must follow the teachings of the Bible.

On my own, I could care less what people do, but I put the Word first place and so, I teach that we must believe God created man and woman – to fit together perfectly, to love one another, to enjoy this life and to create new life.

God made us. No matter whether we need healing or deliverance, He can take any crooked life and make it straight. If you're struggling in this area, I want you to know that your desires can be completely turned around by the hand of God. Just like any other problem you have, God has made a way of escape for you through His Son, Jesus Christ.

The first step to be free from sexual confusion is to recognize and accept that you are not a mistake and that any deviancy from God's original plan for your body isn't God's plan for you. If God made you a girl, His plan was for you to marry a guy one day and create new life – that's how the world keeps on going. The devil just got in and caused confusion somewhere. He's the author of confusion, remember?

Even though we might not understand all the particulars, as Christians we must make God's Word the final authority on everything, including controversial subjects like this one. Unlike man's current theories, the Word of God does not change. It is the *"Same yesterday, today and forever"* (Hebrews 13:8).

Once you accept the Word of God as the final authority on the subject, the next step is to develop a will to change. In other words, you must want to give up the lifestyle. This isn't easy if you've come to find solace in a group, but after the initial decision to make that change is done, you will want to reinforce your decision by diving into the things of God.

If you are not already, begin to pray and read your Bible daily and find a church to attend that preaches the uncompromised Word of God. Find a program to help you if you are struggling, but get into the habit of depending on the Word as your final authority. Let God's love wash through you and reveal Himself to you in a greater way. Pray for God to increase your will to change and become more like Him.

When you pray, I encourage you to ask the Holy Spirit to reveal the roots of the spiritual, mental and emotional issues that led you to the desires or the lifestyle. It's easier to conquer what you can identify. God loves you. He'll show you how to do what you need to do in order to be completely healed, step-by-step.

Everybody Is Different

Remember, everyone is different and there are many ways that Satan deceives us into thinking we are something we're not. Again, he is the author of confusion in every area of our lives, including sexuality, and will try to destroy God's kids by bringing confusion any way he can. Whether its adulterous relationships, fornication, homosexuality, or anything sexual that God has told us in His Word isn't good for us, we can overcome it through our reliance on Jesus Christ.

Jesus can cut through all the confusion in an instant and show us our true nature and our true path in life. And it all begins with a close, personal relationship with Him. The more you get to know Him, the more you'll see that He only wants the best for you. His nature will start rubbing off on you – a nature that is loving, joyful, merciful, free and holy.

If your conscience isn't sharp because you've never had much teaching on the holiness of God, the Lord will help to sharpen your conscience so that you immediately know what is right and wrong as situations arise. Just ask Him for help. Between His still small voice and the Word that you'll be reading each day, you're going to have all the inner ammunition you need to combat temptation and live free!

With God's help, you can release the situations and people that have been hindering your success with God and become the free and happy person He created you to be.

CHAPTER 15

Never Stray Away from Your Personal Convictions

It's fun being saved today. There is so much to do and so much opportunity. There's no need to feel cheated by not living a sinful life. But, when I was a teenager, my parents went to a church that preached that just about everything was a sin – baseball, the radio, television. What they preached against the most was women! Women couldn't wear makeup or pants because it was "sin" in their eyes. They wore long dresses and looked as plain as possible. As a teenager, I figured that the ugliest women in the world went to my church.

I've always been the kind of man that likes makeup on a woman. I tell my wife, "Don't leave home without it." That stuff is great! I like a nice dress and a little flash. If I see my wife all dressed up, I say, "Get down with your bad self, Mama!" I like it.

So, when I was a teenager and my grandmother would start hounding me about dating girls in the church, I developed a line that would just make her beg for the rapture.

"Why don't you date one of the girls in the church?" my grandmother would ask.

"Oh, no, Grandma, I am going amongst the Philistines. I am a Samson boy, myself! I want a Delilah. I like mine a little dirty!"

She'd start sucking wind and say, "Oh, Lawd! Take me now!"

I'd say, "Take her, Lord, take her."

Grandma's Donut in the Swimming Pool

My grandmother never cut her hair, and it always looked like she was wearing a big donut to me because she wound yards of the stuff into a bun on top of her head. That bun was huge. When I was a boy, I figured that if she went swimming, she'd never be able to dive under the water because that big bun on her head would keep her afloat. I figured she'd hit the water and go whap! That donut wasn't going anywhere!

As she grew older, her hair got thinner and the bun wasn't as big, but I remember watching her take her hair down once. It was almost to her knees.

"Grandma!" I said, and she knew what I meant.

"Oh, I will never cut my hair," she told me. There was no way she was cutting her hair because the church told her it was sin. It wasn't, of course, but she didn't cut that hair. When they buried Grandma, they made sure to wrap that long hair up tight and she went to the grave with that big, heavy bun on her head. I don't think the angels would have recognized her without it! Saint Peter would have probably had to look twice at the roll!

As I stood staring at her in the coffin, I saw that Grandma's big bun was cocking her chin down a bit. I whispered to my mama, "Mama, y'all need to get rid of that donut. Grandma looks a little uncomfortable, even being dead."

That's a true story. Grandma was a beautiful woman – small, with delicate features, bright blue eyes and silvery white hair – but, that donut sat on top of her head for her whole life. Why? Church tradition. Grandma went to a church that focused on personal convictions. People were dying and going to Hell all over our town, but the sermon of the week was about women cutting their hair. It was crazy.

Some of those women should have cut their hair. It looked horrible. It weighed a ton and some of them complained of headaches, but they'd never cut it. They'd just snip the ends, which I thought was ridiculous. Cutting is cutting.

I believe Grandma could have been a whole lot more comfortable in her life if she'd switched to another church! Maybe one that spent more time preserving truth instead of focusing on slashing what they considered to be false? Maybe one that didn't preach personal convictions? I believe that would have suited old Grandma well…and made her sit a little straighter, too. I'm convinced that the hump on her back had something to do with that big, old, heavy bun!

Are You Saved Just Enough to Be Miserable?

I have seen some miserably saved people in my years of ministry! I'm talking about sad and disgusted Christians, but I'm not one of them! I'm not saved just enough to be miserable. I live according to the Word and my personal convictions – not what other people feel convicted for. That's freedom in Jesus.

God never told us that we had to do exactly what the person next to us does. If we live by other people's rules, we'll be miserable. But, if we stick by God's rules and the convictions of our own heart, we'll be happy. It's just that simple.

To me, there is nothing better than knowing Jesus. There is nothing better than being able to reach out to Him at any time and receive His joy, His peace and His love. I also rely on His divine counsel. When I need direction in my ministry or in my personal life, it's a relief to have Jesus on my side because I know I can always rely on Him to show me what I need to do. The Lord is always right here, ready and willing to honor my faith.

I'm a Blunt Man When It Comes to Faith

Faith is important because it's part of God's system. Believing is what God requires us to do in order to receive from Him. The Bible defines faith like this: *"Now faith is the substance of things hoped for, the evidence of things not seen"* (Hebrews 11:1). I like to say that when I can't see it, that's my evidence that it's there. So, I just thank Him for it...even though I can't see it yet. That may sound crazy to the natural mind, but it's God's way of thinking and it produces results.

I'm a blunt man. I'm the kind of man who wants to know the bottom line. If my staff comes up to me with a situation, I don't want to hear a long and drawn-out story of the who's, why's and how's. I say, "Tell me the bottom line first. Tell me where I stand first, and then, you can go back and tell me the particulars of the situation if I need to hear it."

I'm the same way with faith. I don't have to know all the particulars of how faith works, I know its God's plan of getting something to me. When I read His Word, I know I must believe it and not doubt it if I want results. I know that when I apply my own belief to something God said, I'm on my way to seeing whatever I need in the natural come to pass.

When I first got saved, I had a little trouble because none of the religious people around me really believed by faith. They preached the Word and prayed, but few that I knew really believed in anything past salvation. When I started reading the Bible, I took everything God said as truth. His Word was something I could trust. If He said it, I believed it and made no provisions for failure concerning it. Consequently, God moved quickly in my life.

I wasn't religious enough yet to start doubting. And, when I'd say something that the Bible said about healing or another controversial subject, I often got long-winded speeches from other church people. They wanted to "explain" what God really meant. As they talked, I realized that they were trying to show me all the good points of *not* believing what God said...and I didn't want to do that!

Back then, I'd never heard anybody preach that you could have what the Bible said you could have; I didn't know the name of one "faith" teacher. But I decided that if I was going to be saved, then I was going to believe what God said. I never really struggled with a lot of the doubts other Christians I knew struggled with. They'd bring up philosophical arguments all the time. They'd pose their questions to me and I'd just say, "Well, what did God say about it? If He said I shouldn't do it anymore in His Word, then I'm not doing it anymore!"

Simple, blunt and to the point, was how I responded to the long-winded religious debating of my early years as a Christian. I'd say, "Man, I was lost when He found me, and it's been nothing but uphill since He dragged me out of that velvet sewer I used to play rock music in! Why should I start arguing with God now? He made me. He knows what's best. And, He put it all down on paper for me right in the Bible so I wouldn't have to wonder."

I wasn't interested in condemning people for what *they* didn't believe, I was trying to get them to stop condemning me for what I believed – which was simply the Word of God! I was interested in encouraging people, not condemning them. I had enough condemnation in the world and I sure wasn't looking for it in the church. So, because people couldn't find a good argument with me, they'd move on to somebody else. They were always looking for somebody to debate the scriptures with them.

I don't enjoy debating with people. The Word is the final authority, but if a situation isn't black-and-white in the Word, then I believe that it's up to each of us to personally seek God about the situation and decide what we're going to do – to receive His counsel. That's where your own personal convictions come into play.

People have always tried to get me to live according to their personal convictions, to get me to believe their way. But, I've got convictions of my own and I want to believe God's way! I say, "Look, let me live according to the Word. Let me live according to my faith in God to do what He said. And, if it goes beyond that, then let me live according to my personal convictions."

There are some things I am against strongly but because they're not in the Bible, I don't go around preaching to people about them. That would be preaching my personal convictions, and my convictions might not be applicable to everyone else. I may share what I believe, but I don't preach it like Gospel truth because it just isn't Gospel truth.

"Do You Believe in Drinking, Brother Jesse?"

I've made a decision to live my life a certain way, the way God has convicted me to live. Take drinking alcohol for instance.

A man asked me the other day. He said, "Do you believe in drinking alcohol?" I said, "No."

"Why?"

"I don't want my Holy Spirit to get tipsy."

"Yeah, but I mean, what does it matter if you have a little of this and a little of that?"

"It all starts with a little," I said.

You see, before I was saved, I was a heavy drinker and drug user. God delivered me from that. So, why would I want to go back to that? That life was sending me to Hell, and there is nothing in Hell that I want. I'm not looking for ways to turn back. I'm looking for ways to go forward – and the further away I get from my old life the better!

I've got a good friend that started drinking a glass of wine every now and again a long time ago.

"Just a little wine," his doctor told him, "it's good for his blood."

His doctor told him to do it, but God warned my friend against it. He told me that God softly spoke to his heart: "Don't mess with that stuff. You've got a problem with that. Remember that. Remember when I saved you from it."

But my friend didn't listen to the voice of God and, instead, chose to side with the doctor. Today, he is an alcoholic. He has called me and talked with me about it. He has cried on the phone and said things like, "I just don't understand why I'm so bound by this thing."

A lot of people want to use scripture to justify drinking even when the Lord has already warned them against it. They usually use this scripture: *"Drink no longer water, but use a little wine for thy stomach's sake and thine often infirmities"* (1 Timothy 5:23). But there are some people that can't take any wine at all, for any sake! Why? Because they don't know how to handle it to start with and it's a weakness for them. It is a personal conviction for them and to do it would be to sin.

You see, whatever you know is a weakness for you is something you should stay away from completely. It may not be considered biblical sin, but it is definitely something that you should steer away from.

Never Sway from Your Personal Convictions

When Paul the Apostle was writing Romans chapter fourteen, he had personal convictions on his mind. He mainly dealt with food because that was a serious source of irritation between Jewish believers. What was considered clean and unclean was a huge deal to Jewish believers and Paul was interested in sharing reasons why they should avoid arguments and respect one another's personal convictions.

> For one believeth that he may eat all things: another, who is weak, eateth herbs.
> Let not him that eateth despise him that eateth not; and let not him which eateth not judge him that eateth: for God hath received him.

Who art thou that judgest another man's servant? to his own master he standeth or falleth. Yea, he shall be holden up: for God is able to make him stand.

One man esteemeth one day above another: another esteemeth every day alike. Let every man be fully persuaded in his own mind.

Romans 14:2-5

Paul was saying that we should go about living our life according to our faith in God's Word – according to whatever we are fully persuaded in our own minds that God has told us to do.

Other People's Convictions

But why dost thou judge thy brother? or why dost thou set at nought thy brother? for we shall all stand before the judgment seat of Christ.

For it is written, As I live, saith the Lord, every knee shall bow to me, and every tongue shall confess to God.

So then every one of us shall give account of himself to God.

Let us not therefore judge one another any more: but judge this rather, that no man put a stumblingblock or an occasion to fall in his brother's way.

Romans 14:10-13

When we judge another person's personal convictions unto God, we're wasting our time because we won't be their final judge.

That's God's job! Everybody is going to give an account of what they've done here on the earth; so we don't have to execute judgment on them any earlier.

Because the Jews had such strict rules about what was good to eat and what wasn't good to eat, Paul wanted to shed some light on the issue. He wanted people to know that nothing was unclean unto itself, but it was up to the individual to decide what was clean and unclean to him. It was about personal conviction.

> *I know, and am persuaded by the Lord Jesus, that there is nothing unclean of itself: but to him that esteemeth any thing to be unclean, to him it is unclean.*
>
> *But if thy brother be grieved with thy meat, now walkest thou not charitably. Destroy not him with thy meat, for whom Christ died.*
>
> *Let not then your good be evil spoken of:*
>
> *For the kingdom of God is not meat and drink; but righteousness, and peace, and joy in the Holy Ghost.*
>
> *For he that in these things serveth Christ is acceptable to God, and approved of men.*
>
> **Let us therefore follow after the things which make for peace, and things wherewith one may edify another.**
>
> Romans 14:14-19

Paul stressed the importance of following after peace and doing the things that will lift other people up instead of tearing them down. He said, *"Hast thou faith? have it to thyself before God. Happy is he that condemneth not himself in that thing which he alloweth"* (Romans 14:22).

In other words, if you've got faith enough to eat one thing, then do it and stop trying to condemn those who don't eat like you. Stop trying to condemn other people for what portions of the Word they've got faith for and just encourage them.

That does not mean you should stop encouraging people with the Word and with your faith. By all means, we should share God's Word with one another! It just means that you shouldn't criticize people for their personal convictions or judge them for where they are in God. Never use the Word to cut somebody down; use the Word to heal and restore them and to give them wisdom to live well.

Whatsoever Is Not of Faith

Paul closes the chapter with a statement that I believe is as blunt and to the point as it gets! He said, *"And he that doubteth is damned if he eat, because he eateth not of faith: **for whatsoever is not of faith is sin"*** (Romans 14:23). Wow! Whatever isn't faith is sin?

When I first read that scripture I thought it sounded harsh but I'm a bottom line man and I understand what Paul was saying. He is saying, 'Look, whatever a person is convicted of and has faith to do, he should do it. If he doesn't, then he is sinning.' It's about missing the mark.

While it seems harsh to say, *"...**for whatsoever is not of faith is sin"*** according to the Bible, it's true. In fact, there is a verse in Hebrews 11:6 that says, *"But without faith it is impossible to please him: for he that cometh to God must believe that He is, and that he* *is a rewarder of them that diligently seek Him."*

It's impossible to please God without faith. Whatever isn't of faith is sin. That must mean that if something is not faith, then it must be sin. It's pretty black-and-white. That's the reason why I believe in faith. I have to because if I don't, I'm missing the mark. I'm sinning and I don't want to sin against God. That's strong, but hey, it's what the Bible says. Don't get mad at me!

IF you can "handle it"

why are you having so much trouble

shaking it?

Recognizing Your Need for GOD

Realizing What Nailed Jesus to the Cross

CHAPTER 16

Beware of Being Independent of Your Maker

You *can* live without recognizing God, but it's really no way to live. It's just plain miserable. There is no goodness outside of God. If you convince yourself that there is, you've just allowed the devil to deceive you. In fact, the Bible says, *"The fool hath said in his heart, There is no God. They are corrupt, they have done abominable works, there is none that doeth good"* (Psalm 14:1).

If you've chosen to recognize God as your Maker, then you're the opposite of a fool. You're a wise person. Why not walk in more wisdom and stop "x-ing" God out of certain parts of your life? Why not talk to Him when you're struggling instead of keeping the thoughts to yourself? After all, He can help you out.

Your Maker can guide you into all truth. He can develop your character so that you'll know the reasons *why* it's not good to be independent from Him. God can help you to resist temptation in many different ways, if you let Him. He will show you what works for you.

Too many people think that they can handle temptation without God. You may assume that you can handle what you're playing with. Don't let the devil deceive you. Be honest with yourself. **You can't handle it.**

That thing has a hook on the end that keeps tugging at you. If you can handle it on your own, why are you having so much trouble with it? Why can't you seem to shake the craving? Let the elevator go to the top!

God doesn't have a list of things you can and can't talk to Him about. He doesn't say, "No, you weak puppy! I don't have time to mess with that. Deal with it on your own!" No, if it's causing you to stumble, it's important to Him. If it's causing your mind to be filled with restlessness or anything else that isn't good, it's important to Him.

Besides, it won't be the first time He has heard about it. He has been watching you struggle the whole time, just waiting for you to call on Him for help and for you to fight the impulse with your faith. Man, you can't surprise God! Your darkest "secret" isn't a secret to Him. He already knows about it, and He already has a plan to rid you of it. But, for you to walk in that plan, you're going to have to, first, open up to Him and talk about it.

God is the sweeper of your soul, but if you are always stealing the broom and trying to do your own cleaning because you think you can handle it, I've got news for you. You're going to live in some serious slop!

God is omnipotent and omnipresent. He's "omni" all the way! Everywhere at once! Able to handle any problem you can think up. You aren't taking up His precious time, because He lives above and beyond time. He is forever. He is a Spirit, and if you've chosen Him, then He's living in you. Talk to Him. He's waiting.

The more you realize that He's with you and there for you, the easier it will be to resist when the temptation to sin is strong. You can say "no" to anything you want to say "no" to. You aren't powerless. But, you will need God's help if sin or the temptation to sin has its hooks in your mind, will and emotions.

Jesus Wasn't Crucified with Nails, Jesus Was Crucified with Sin

Nails were driven into Jesus' body, but they weren't what really crucified Him on the cross. Jesus was crucified, not by nails, but by sin. It was sin that beat Him until He was unrecognizable. It was sin that made Him carry His own cross. Sin stripped Jesus of His clothes and threw dice for them. Sin drove the nails in His wrists and feet, forced a crown of thorns on His head and humiliated Him with sarcasm and spit.

Who crucified Jesus? Pilot crucified Jesus by his cowardice; Judas, by his love of money; The high priest, by his love of power; The Pharisees, by their self-righteousness; and the mob, by their preference for Barabbas.

What did *you* crucify Jesus with? You see, everyone has done something. *"For all have sinned, and come short of the glory of God"* (Rom. 3:23). What have you done? What sin in your life put Jesus on the cross? I hope you're getting my point.

Redemption came at a great expense. Christ suffered so that you wouldn't have to. He hung your sin on His body so that you could get rid of sin today. Jesus was weighted down with the sins, not just of you and of me, but of the *world*. Imagine the pressure and darkness of all that sin. It's the weight of sin that held Him to the cross.

Pilot, Judas, the high priest, the Pharisees, the mob, you and me – no matter what we've done, it was our sin that Jesus paid the price for. Let that sink in to your spirit, because the more personal Jesus becomes to you, the greater your capacity to say "no" when the devil or your own human flesh comes calling.

Thinking, Saying and Doing

The devil is a liar. He wants to remind you of everything you *don't* have. He wants to make you discontent with yourself, God and everything in this world, but the Bible tells you not to listen to his lies and to simply rejoice in the Lord always.

> *Rejoice in the Lord alway: and again I say, Rejoice.*
> *Let your moderation be known unto all men. The Lord is at hand.*
> *Be careful for nothing; but in every thing by prayer and supplication with thanksgiving let your requests be made known unto God.*
> *And the peace of God, which passeth all understanding, shall keep your hearts and minds through Christ Jesus.*
> *Finally, brethren, whatsoever things are true, whatsoever things are honest, whatsoever things are just, whatsoever things are pure, whatsoever things are lovely, whatsoever things are of good report; if there be any virtue, and if there be any praise, think on these things.*
> *Those things, which ye have both learned, and received, and heard, and seen in me, do: and the God of peace shall be with you.*
>
> Philippians 4:4-9

Notice that this passage starts with joy – rejoice! Before God lets us know what to think about, God gives you what you should be doing and saying. In other words, He wants you to talk and act by faith. You don't conjure up the thoughts first; you say what God says first. You act like God acts. It's done by faith.

Before you've even convinced your own mind, God tells you to praise Him with your mouth. Don't let one day go by without rejoicing and giving God thanks for what He's done for you. Gratitude is important. It jerks some reality into your mind and lets you know life is not all bad! God has done some good things! Don't let the devil lie to you and deceive you into thinking otherwise.

Notice it didn't say, "Rejoice only when everything is going your way." No, it says, rejoice *always*. Another scripture says that we offer up a "sacrifice of praise" (Hebrews 13:15). Sometimes it's not easy to praise God in the midst of trouble – sometimes it's a sacrifice to your own natural tendency to feel sorry for yourself. Verse five tells you to *do* something – be moderate. The Bible tells you to be so moderate that everybody around you notices. Obviously, God cares about your reputation and wants you to be a good witness for Him.

Next, verse six tells you not to worry about everything so much – stop letting the devil stress you out. He wants you so bound up by stress and confusion that you lose all joy. Don't give him the pleasure of seeing you down in the dumps all the time. Instead, listen to this scripture from God and be careful for nothing.

What are you supposed to do about the problem then? Verse six tells you that too! It says that if you've got a problem, you should do the following things: (1) pray about it, (2) request what you need from God, and (3) be thankful for what He's already done in your life. This is the life of faith. Then, in verse seven, God tells you what will happen if you do this – you will have peace.

When you're praising Him, praying and making your requests known to Him, being moderate and not worrying about everything, the peace of God will *"keep"* your heart and mind stable. That peace will protect your mind and heart. You'll have so much peace, it'll blow your mind! Your intellect won't even be able to grasp it. I'm talking about the peace that surpasses all understanding!

Next, God gives you a whole list of stuff to focus your mind on. You see, God made you and He knows your mind doesn't stop for too long. It's got to be thinking about something, so He told you what you should allow to stay in your mind. Thoughts come and go, but the ones to focus on are the ones that are good and you know they're good thoughts if they pass the test. Is the thought true? Honest? Just? Pure? Lovely? Is it good news? Does it have virtue? Is the thought worthy of praise? Notice that God gives you all positive words to test your thoughts. He doesn't want you focusing on negative things at all.

Lastly, the scripture tells you to focus your mind on the things you've learned, received, heard and seen *in* Jesus. Buddy, when you start focusing on what you've learned from Jesus, you're not going to focus on the negative. If you start zoning in on what you've received from Him, you're going to be filled with gratitude. If you remind yourself of what you've heard and seen, God, who is full of peace, will flood you with exactly what you need to live above the cares of this life.

CHAPTER 17

The Purity of the Gospel
The Pollution of Sin

Sin isn't just an act, it's also a decision of the heart. Things like adultery, stealing and killing are just the effects of a *heart-condition*.

I don't like to complicate the issue of sin and temptation in my own life. For me, everything boils down to the decision I made when I said, "Jesus, come into my life…" When I accepted Jesus as my Savior, I accepted His teachings too. If God said it and I'm now born again, I'm going to believe the Bible and act on it to the best of my knowledge and ability. That was my decision and I'm not interested in going back on it.

I've got personal convictions that I can't go back on. I've made decisions that there are some things I will never, ever do again. Before I was saved, I took trips and never left my house. The drugs I took had me flying with the birds, buddy! I didn't care if somebody told me, "You could die on those drugs." I'd say, "OK" It didn't make a difference to me. I accepted the fact that the stuff could kill me and decided to do it anyway. Even as a heathen, I had convictions. They were warped, but they were there!

I decided early on in my life that if I did something, it was going to be because I *wanted* to do something. I ran my life and took the responsibility for my life. Before I came to the knowledge of Jesus,

I never saw an ugly woman in my life. When you're drinking night and day, they just don't exist! Nothing cures a woman's ugliness like being drunk. If I got drunk enough, a one-legged monkey started looking good!

But, when Jesus came into my life, He said, "Now I am going to let the purity of the Gospel go in you as far as the pollution of sin." I was changed on the inside and it effected what I did. Suddenly, I *wanted* to read my Bible. I *wanted* to go to church. I *wanted* to pray and get close to God, because I wanted the relationship with Him more than I wanted the high of drugs.

If God Changed Me, He Can Change You

In the beginning of my walk with the Lord, Christians would tell me, "Now, Brother Jesse, don't get around booze because, since you drank so much, it will really pull on you." That might have been true for some people, but it wasn't true for me. I could have worked at a whiskey factory and it wouldn't have made a difference because, you see, **I was born again**. I had shaken what had once held me bound.

You see, the man that used to do those things died! I was birthed into the kingdom of the Highest God, and the desires that lived in me before didn't have a place anymore. I was clean, and I didn't ever want to be unclean again. I was free, and I wasn't looking to be bound again. From then on, all I was looking for was more of Him.

I was like an innocent child in that I'd just read the Word and said, "Wow!" I had no problem believing it. Now, sometimes I'd read a hard scripture and wonder why God would ever say that, but I never doubted that it was true or that it was the right thing to do. I had faith in God and knew He was just going to have to help me if He wanted me to do some of that stuff!

Sometimes I'd get to a scripture like, "Love your brother" and I'd laugh to myself and say, "God, you don't *know* my brother! If you knew my brother you'd take that scripture right out the Bible!" I'd read, "Pray for those that despitefully use you" and say, "Wait a minute, God. If you get *rid* of those that despitefully use you, then they will never despitefully use you again!" I'd read, "Bless those that curse you" and say, "Just one good punch and then they will never be able to cuss you again!"

I'd laugh as I read some of them because they seemed so hard to do, but I took them at face value and said, "Well, I guess I'll be doing this now." I wasn't always successful but I was on my way! The point is that I made a decision and I wasn't looking back. This is all you have to do too. Dive into your relationship with God and there won't be room for anything else. Get close to Him and He will purify you from the inside out so that you don't even *want* the pollution of your former life.

You Get What You Believe For

The Bible is so simple. It takes a good theologian to help you misunderstand it. The basics of faithful Christian living are right there in black-and-white, and all you've got to do is believe it. God does the work; you do the *faith*. You get what you believe for.

Jesus said, *"For with what judgment ye judge, ye shall be judged:*

and with what measure ye mete, it shall be measured to you again"
(Matthew 7:2). In other words, whatever measurement you use to
judge somebody else is the measurement that is going to be used
to judge you. In Luke 6:38 it says, *"Give, and it shall be given
unto you; good measure, pressed down, and shaken together, and
running over, shall men give into your bosom. For with the same
measure that ye mete withal it shall be measured to you again."*
There is that measurement thing again.

In other words, you determine how much you'll receive by how
much you are giving – whether that is financially, physically or
spiritually. It's the law of sowing and reaping and it works in
every part of life – including faith. What you believe, you will
receive. What you doubt, you will do without. You've already got
a measure of faith that was given to you by God. How much you
use it is up to you.

I've decided that I am simply going to use my faith and believe
what I read in the Bible. I believe scriptures that say that I am a son
of God, and, as a son, I'm a joint heir with Jesus Christ. I confess
the Word of God over myself.

Confessing the Word Over Your Own Life

I put myself in the scriptures because it builds my faith. This is
a habit of mine that keeps me strong. It'll do the same for you.
You see, the Word is called a "sword" in the Bible and it's good
for cutting the devil to shreds! It's also good for cutting negativity
out of your mind. People will cut you down and make you feel like
a low-down, dirty dog from Hell, but God will lift you up and show

you the way to live a heavenly life, right here on earth.

When I build myself up by confessing the Word, I say things like, "I'm more than a conqueror! If God be for me, who can be against me? I'm the workmanship of God, created in Christ. Old things have passed away, and I've become new! I am in Christ and all power and dominion has been given to me! Blessings come upon me, so much so that they overtake me! I'm a lender and not a borrower. I'm blessed in the city and blessed in the field, I'm blessed when I go in and I'm blessed when I go out!"

I may even just stand in front of my bathroom mirror and preach to myself saying, "If the enemy comes at me in one direction, he will flee from me in seven! No weapon formed against me will prosper! I'm God's property, bought with the blood of Jesus and free from every curse of the law. Sin, sickness, poverty, fear, doubt, worry, confusion and all the devil's works do not have dominion on me! I've been given the spirit of wisdom and revelation so that I may know God better and I'm being made perfect in every good work to do God's will! I'm blessed with all spiritual blessings in Christ Jesus! I'm prosperous and in good health because my soul prospers!"

I go further when I need more, saying something like, "God supplies all my needs. He makes my way prosperous and gives me good success. God has given me the ability to produce wealth and confirm His covenant in the earth. His favor surrounds me like a shield! He is increasing me a thousand times and blessing me as He has promised and there is no good thing that He will withhold from me. Why? Because I walk uprightly and besides that...He just loves me!"

Whew! Now, that's what the Word says about me! Don't get mad at me because I choose to believe it. I didn't write it, I just chose to accept it by faith. I'm recognizing the power of the cross. I'm receiving that from God on a daily basis and not just a church service basis. God loves me; He just can't help Himself. And, I love Him; I just can't help myself! I've chosen to believe His Word about me and not believe what the world says I am. You should do the same thing. If you don't build yourself up, who is going to do it for you? There is power in the Word, and if you grab a hold of it, nobody is going to be able to tear it loose from your heart.

Don't Let Anybody Fill You with Doubt

The first few years after I was born again, people were always trying to convince me that I couldn't be what God said I could be. When that happened, I just tuned them right out. I've continued to do that since the day I got saved. I've got too much Word in me to accept less than the best. I don't argue with people because you just can't put a mind-of-Christ concept in a natural mind full of doubt. But, I refuse to accept their negative words about me.

I didn't condemn people for not believing God's Word for themselves, but I sure wasn't going to let them move me off of God's Word. While it would discourage me that more people didn't really believe, I was never discouraged by God. His Word continually edged me on to higher faith. And, the closer I got to Him, the more inspiration He'd give me about simply believing Him.

I had people tell me, "You believe like this preacher" or "You believe like that preacher," and I'd say, "No, I just believe what God said." Sometimes that would irritate them. I was just a baby Christian and my diapers were on pretty tight. But, I knew what I believed!

It's Not Denial, It's Simple Faith

Now, I didn't deny what I saw. I still believe the same way today. If sickness tries to attach itself to a believer, I don't deny that it exists. I just deny its right to stay! I don't deny that a person may be depressed, but I do deny the depression's right to stay in a person of God – we have access to His peace, His joy and His love.

Everything we need spiritually, physically, emotionally and financially can be found in the presence of God and in the application of His Word. If we have faith and apply the Word, whatever we need from God will be routed to us. It's coming from God to us, an answer to prayer in response to faith in His Word.

If somebody was sick, it was just a fact! But it wasn't the truth. The truth is that God said, *"...I am the LORD that healeth thee"* (Exodus 15:26). The truth is Psalm 103:2-3: *"Bless the LORD, O my soul, and forget not all His benefits: Who forgiveth all thine iniquities; who healeth all thy diseases."* The truth is Isaiah 53:5, *"But He was wounded for our transgressions, He was bruised for our iniquities: the chastisement of our peace was upon Him; and with His stripes we are healed."*

If someone in the church was broke, it was just a fact! But, it wasn't the truth. The truth is that God has made a way for our prosperity by giving and following after His righteousness, but if we don't obey Him, we're not going to see it come to pass His way.

The truth is Proverbs 11:25, *"The generous soul will be made* rich, and he who waters will also be watered himself." The truth is Proverbs 21:21, *"He that followeth after righteousness and mercy findeth life, righteousness, and honour."* The truth is that if we sow, we will reap like Mark 4:8 says, *"And other fell on good ground, and did yield fruit that sprang up and increased; and brought forth, some thirty, and some sixty, and some an hundred."*

God says, *"I lead in the way of righteousness, in the midst of the paths of judgment: That I may cause those that love me to inherit substance; and I will fill their treasures"* (Proverbs 8:20-21).

So, I don't deny that the devil plagues us with his hellish sicknesses, diseases or poverty, but I have made a decision that there is nothing in Hell that I want! Jesus died to free us from all that hellish junk – and the blood of Jesus is enough! God doesn't send sickness to teach me something; it's just a product of a sin-altered world. If sickness was of God, Heaven would be full of it, but it's not. There is no poverty or sickness in Heaven, so we can refuse the temptation to give in to that junk here on earth.

Sometimes people confuse themselves about faith. It's not about living in denial, it's about believing God's Word to such a degree that you see what the devil is doing. And, because you know what God has said, you know God's Word will prevail!

The Devil Has No Right to Steal, Kill and Destroy

He does it, but he doesn't have a right to. You enforce his defeat when you stand on God's Word and remind that idiot of the power of the cross. The bottom line is that the power of God is stronger than the power of the devil – and all the promises of God are inherited through both faith and patience.

When church people in my early days said that I had to sin every day, I'd say, "No I don't. You may, but I don't. I'm born again and my sin nature died! I've got a faith nature. I'm a believer! I'm not a sinner anymore. I'm made righteous by the blood of Jesus!"

When they said sickness was just a part of life, I'd say, "The Bible says Jesus took my infirmity. By His stripes I was healed! If He took my infirmity, why would I want it? And, if He bore my sickness, why should I have it? If God wanted us to throw up, He'd say 'thou shalt throw up!' Jesus went around healing people, not touching them and giving them sickness." They would get irritated with me, but I was just telling them what God said. I just simply believed the Bible.

Now, that was a very simple way of thinking, but I believe that God wants us to have childlike faith in God's Word. I think He wants us to believe Him! If you really want to get into "deep things of God," you are going to have to begin by believing God's Word like a child. You've got to get past having pride in your intellect. Start with the basics of simple, Christian living and work your way up.

Be a **Doer**

Release Pride

Protect

your household of Faith

Rid Yourself of Unholy Ambition

CHAPTER 18

Unholy Ambition

When I was a kid, I played football for this coach who was determined to have the best team each football season. In those days, I could run like a rabbit. I was too small and the other players would hit me and knock me over the line. But, this coach could have cared less and he had a saying that he'd holler out during practice.

"Hit, lift and drive!"

One day, while we were practicing, the coach looked at me and said, "Boy, I don't care if you are 130 pounds and the other guy is 210. You run up his nose and beat his brains out, you understand me?"

"OK coach!"

This coach would make you run until you threw up! I'm not kidding! I saw some guy throw up and he said, "Suck it up, boy!" That's gross, but it's the truth.

He made a pen that we called "the bull pen." It had three wooden beams running one way, and three wooden beams running the other way and corner beams to hold it together. He would put one guy on defense and one guy on offense. Then, he would stand over you and say, "I want you to hit and I only want to see one of you come up. I want to see some blood!"

So, the guys on the team would do everything they could to show some blood without hurting themselves too much. When the coach would yell, "Hit!" we'd pop pimples and do everything we could to look mean!

At sixteen, you've got so many pimples that when you go to a pizza place and they ask, "How do you want your pizza?" You say, "Look at this" and point to your face, "Right here. Check that out. That is exactly how I want it." Most kids have a face that looks like pepperoni pizza at that age.

I will never forget that coach, though. He was hard. But he was wrong for being so hard. He hated every other football team. Actually, they fired him after two boys died. They were completely exhausted – one had a heart attack and the other went into a coma. I don't know what ever happened as far as that, because, in those days, we weren't told he was let go because of the two boys. Everything was kept very hush-hush but everybody on that team knew what killed those boys – and we felt lucky to be alive!

There were many practices where I felt like I was going to die! I didn't go into a coma but I wanted to – anything to stop running! Why would that coach push us to go beyond what was good for our bodies? Because he coveted the top spot. He wanted to have the best team, and he was willing to hurt people in order to have it. It taught me a valuable lesson about ambition that has gone too far and how pride can warp a man's dreams.

Unholy Ambition in the Ministry

Pride is everywhere. It's in the business world, in marriages and even in the church. Why is it everywhere? Because the devil is always out and he is consumed with pride and, what I like to call, "unholy ambition."

One of the most phenomenal evangelists of this age is Dr. Billy Graham. I owe my soul to this man because it was Dr. Graham who preached on television in 1974 – who spent the money to buy the airtime, just for the purpose of telling the good news. I watched him and he introduced me to a man named Jesus Christ – and my life has never been the same.

Later, after God called me into the ministry, I'd often hear other preachers criticize Dr. Billy Graham by saying, "He is so simple." It would anger me. The salvation message is simple. Jesus made sure of it! He doesn't want people to have to jump through hoops!

So, I'd defend Dr. Graham and say, "Well, are you filling up football stadiums? That man has touched more people for Jesus than anybody I know and that's as deep as you can get, man! It's so deep that he made it simple, and that's how I got born again. I simply accepted a simple scripture he quoted. And it was so deep, it literally caused me to lose my mind and gain the mind of Christ!" John 3:16 will do that to you!

There are so many Christians out there who think they're so deep. They can't fill up their own living room with a Bible study and, yet, they have the audacity to criticize wonderful men of God who are bringing thousands and perhaps millions to the knowledge of Jesus. They're puffed up on pride; they think they've got so much revelation concerning the Word, but they have a hard time hearing the simple things of God. But, it's the simple concepts in God's Word that can create radical changes in life. It doesn't have to be deep to make a difference.

Pride is Satan's Version of Godly Confidence

Pride is Satan's version of a quality that God wants you to have – confidence. In an effort to avoid pride, some people will beat themselves up and end up having virtually no confidence at all. But, you've got to have confidence if you want to do anything in life – including whipping temptation. That's why the Bible is filled with scriptures to build you up and not to tear you down. But, there is such a thing as unholy ambition.

When you've got ambition, you've got a strong desire to achieve something. You've got a goal and you're working towards it. There is nothing wrong with having ambition in life. It's good and you need it to be successful. But, there is a point where ambition goes too far. When a person is willing to compromise their principles to get where they want to be, that's what I call unholy ambition.

Ambition and holiness can seem like polar opposites, but they are not. You can be both ambitious and holy. Holiness isn't unattainable. It doesn't mean shutting yourself off from society or walking around in a daze and saying prayers all day. Being holy simply means that you're dedicated to living a pure and morally upright life.

When you've decided to live a holy life, it means that you've made a commitment to God – you're consecrated to Him and are living according to His principles. But, when your ambition outweighs your holiness, that's when you've got a problem. When you begin to do everything on your own and leave God out of the picture, that's when you've got even more problems!

This is a pride issue and it's at odds against the things of God.

Pride and unholy ambition is exactly what got the devil kicked out of Heaven. So, you can't mix that kind of thing with your Christianity and expect to avoid the deception of the devil.

In ministry, there are a lot of ambitious men and women who have a heart to see God's Word preached throughout the whole earth. They're excited about spreading the Gospel and that's great. We're commanded to be ambitious in this way when we're told in Mark 16:15 to, *"Go ye into all the world, and preach the gospel to every creature."*

But, there are some who lose sight of the reason they're preaching and get caught up in the unholy ambition of works. They just want to pack the church out with people because, the more people sitting in the pews, the more important they feel. They think they're some big dog on the block. This is pride and their motivation is an unholy ambition.

No matter what you do for God, God ought to come first! Your main ambition should be the ambition of the Lord Jesus Christ, which is to reconcile others back to God and not to puff up your own ego. It doesn't matter how many scriptures you know, it's what you apply to your own life that is going to help you.

The Only Big Dog

The only Big Dog is God, and if you're a minister who is puffed up with pride, you're a fool to think that God isn't the real reason that people are filling up the pews in your church. It's the anointing of God that draws people to meetings. That's why when I see a packed church house, I get excited! I am thrilled when people are practically busting the doors down just to get in the church; not because they came to hear my sermon, but because they are hungry for God!

Today's world is filled with entertainment and there is so much going on. People are busier than ever. I don't preach on just the usual church days, I schedule meetings on Mondays, Tuesdays, Thursdays, Fridays and Saturdays too. So, when I see thousands of people clamoring to get in the church on a Monday night, I know they're hungry for God! If they're in church on a Friday night, look out! That service is going to be one power-packed night! They're bringing their faith and it's going to move the hand of God!

I am not trying to be a big preacher. I am not trying to be a big shot. I don't care how many people see me on television because I don't have any of that kind of ambition. I've got one ambition – to touch the world for the Lord.

"No, Jodi, That's Not For You."

Sometimes people around you have an unholy ambition, and if you can, you should try and stop them from affecting you – or your household. If you know about it, get rid of the unholy ambition in your own house.

When my daughter, Jodi, was about sixteen, she used to work at this video store down the street from our house. She'd go out on dates and as she'd leave I'd say to her, "Remember this, there is nothing in Hell you want, girl." Sometimes I'd say, "You know God tells me everything, don't you? If you do something, God will tell me. Just want to let you know that." She'd just look at me like,

Yeah, yeah, yeah. When you're that age, you think you know it all and your parents are idiots – until you need money, of course.

Jodi was a pretty good kid. Man, considering how bad I was as a kid, I thought the girl was just wonderful! I used to go on a date and not come back for three days. They'd find me drunk as a skunk in somebody's swimming pool!

Well, one time this boy came over to my house. He rang the doorbell. I opened the door and looked him up and down. This cat was ugly and looked like a freak. His hair was all over the place and dyed too many shades of ugly. His face looked blotchy and red, and on top of that, he looked like he had an unholy ambition when it came to my daughter. Suddenly, I got a revelation. This kid standing at my door was not sent from God. The devil must have hand plucked this boy just to mess with me. No grandkid of mine was going to look like this super freak.

He said, "Hey, how ya doing?"

I just stood there staring at him. "I am doing good."

"Yeah, I would like to see Jodi."

"You can't," I said and just stood there looking at him.

"Well," he said, "That is her decision."

"No," I said, "It's mine. I'm her father. Bye-bye." I closed the door.

I decided a long time ago to protect my kid – not to overprotect, but to help her out in avoiding the wrong things in life. This kid was a wrong thing. First off, I knew he was from the devil because he rolled on my grass. There was a big slab of cement out there for him to park his heap of a car on, but no – he *had* to roll on my grass.

After I shut the door, Jodi came walking down the stairs. She had heard the doorbell.

"Daddy, was that for me?"

"No, Jodi," I said, "*That* was not for you."

She just looked at me.

"Your Daddy knows what is for you. That was not for you."

Protect Your Kids and Give Them Freedom

The world is full of temptation and teenagers just want freedom to explore the world. I can understand that. Nobody wants to be kept back. Everybody wants to let their wings spread, so to speak, and I understand that. But, it is important to have balance as a parent. Sometimes you let them do what they want, and sometimes you put the brakes on.

Some Christian parents suffocate their kids and never let them make their own decisions or mistakes. I don't believe that's good. What usually happens is that they live so sheltered that when they finally do get out of their parent's grip, they go hog-wild. They are shocked by the world and the devil shows them all the "good stuff" they've been missing out on.

I don't believe in sheltering so much that this kind of thing happens. Sometimes, you just have to let your children do some things in life. I'm not talking about condoning sin or letting them do whatever they want, when they want! I'm talking about letting them breathe and make their own decisions now and again. You should never forget what it was like when you were a teenager. Remember how you felt when you were fifteen or sixteen, how much you wanted to just be in control of your own life. Give your kids a chance to make a choice sometimes.

But also, never stop being a parent. Protect your kids when you can, and tell them how it is out there in the world without harping on them. Be strong for them, so they know they can turn to you for strength when they're feeling down in the dumps. Man, whatever you do, don't become just "the friend." Your kids don't need just another friend. They've probably got plenty of those. They need direction, help and unconditional love. They need somebody they can rely on. They need a real parent.

I told Jodi, "I don't care what mistakes you make. You've always got a home. You've always got a place. Remember that. I may not agree with what you may have done, but I agree with one thing. You are my daughter regardless of what you do. You are the seed of Jesse." I don't believe in cutting your kids off. I do think tough love works with some kids, and sometimes you've got to do it if you've let them run wild for so long that they don't respect you. Mine didn't need it much.

Jodi pulled her shenanigans from time to time, and there were some crazy hormonal years there when I used to joke that she was "emotionally retarded." Those years when she wouldn't go to mailbox without makeup, collected boy-band posters and thought she knew everything…well, they about drove Cathy and I nuts!

We had restrictions, but we gave her freedom too – more than a lot of her Christian friends. Why? Because she'd always been a good kid, and we knew she had to spread those wings a little in the teen years. She might make mistakes, but we had to let her fly a bit and see where she landed.

You see, there's a time to keep the wings clipped. It's called childhood. When the teen years come, it's time to let those wings grow out a little and see where the wings take them. Will they have holy ambition or unholy ambition? If they choose the right route, you commend them and encourage them with words of praise.

If you notice the wings are going in the wrong direction, that's the time to step in and say, "Man, life can really kick you in the head if you don't watch it" and then lay some ground rules. You explain why you believe the way you do. You warn them about life and pray to God they listen to you.

They've Got Free Will Too

Ultimately though, they've got their own free will just like you do. At a certain age, it's up to them to choose what is good or choose what is bad; to choose to follow what you've taught them or not. But we should never forget that while they may look like women and men in the teen years, they are still kids. They still need love and direction. They want it, even if they look like they don't care. They're just too cool sometimes to admit it! You can never go wrong by loving your kid and speaking the truth.

But, don't tell them they're a kid, for goodness sake! They'll hit you with the same argument you gave your parents, "Hey man, I can go to war. I can be sued. I can stay out all night without the police picking me up."

When Jodi would pull this, I'd say what my parents told me, "Well, whoop-de-do! That is no great revelation. Makes no difference to me what your driver's license says. This is my house. When you get your own house, you can have your own house rules and I won't stick my nose in your business. Until then, come in on time."

This book isn't on parenting, so I won't go further, but I will say this: Your kids have to deal with temptation, just like you do. The devil doesn't have any new tricks. When you're strong and know how to combat it, you'll be a good example to your children. Teach them about the love and grace of God, but don't forget to give them the tools you learn for combating temptation and avoiding unholy ambition. Remind them that they don't go through life alone – they need people and they need God.

Be a Doer, Not Just a Talker

Of course, the best thing you can do for yourself and your kids is to be a doer of the Word. If you're a hypocrite, your kids will see it and it won't matter what you say. They'll just hit you with "Well, you do it." If you're looking for an excuse not to obey the Word, your kids will see that and it will affect their opinion of God. They won't feel as compelled to obey God and will even go so far as to find a few scriptures that seem to justify their own sin! If you don't have faith, your kids will question you about it.

The best thing is to build your faith day to day – and let your kids see it. Let them see that you are making a real effort to be a doer. You aren't perfect and your kids won't be perfect either. But, God's grace is there when you mess up. All you have to do is ask for forgiveness. And, if your kids see you lose it or go in the wrong direction, admit to them that you messed up and tell them you're sorry about it. Kids are a lot more forgiving than adults are! They already know you messed up, but it helps them to see that you're teachable too.

Crucify your flesh daily, and not just on Sunday. Use your mouth to combat thoughts. Build yourself up in the Word. Teach your kids the truth that you know and be the best example you know to be of a person who is living by faith, day by day.

A **Religion** without Love

is a **Religion** without power

It fails amid the temptations and conflicts of life

Discover The Power of Love

CHAPTER 19

A Religion Without Love is a Religion Without Power

I once heard a story of a very wealthy man who had a small boy whom he loved dearly. He hired a young lady to help him with his child and tend to the house. Sadly, the young boy died of a disease when he was about five years old. The wealthy man was hurt, brought to his knees and grieved greatly over the death of his child. The lady who had taken care of this little fellow loved him too and suffered silently over the loss of the young boy.

Soon, the man had no more need of the lady in his home. Years went by and the wealthy man went home to be with God. They searched his house and his safety deposit boxes for a will and could not find one. Since he had no heirs, the state came in to auction off his property and all he owned. The man had massive mansions filled with beautiful things and wonderful land with horses. As they began to auction off these things to the highest bidder, a picture of a small boy in an old tattered frame came up. An old lady in the back lifted her hand up to bid.

The auctioneer asked, "What would you bid for this?" He didn't think it was worth more than fifty cents, but she said, "A dollar, I have a dollar." She was a poor lady. No one else bid on the picture and so it was sold for one dollar.

At the end of the auction, when the old lady came to pick up her picture, the man asked, "Why do you want this old picture? The frame is not even worth fifty cents and the picture is tattered." She said, "This was the young son of this man, and I loved that little boy very much. I would like to have a picture of that little fellow. It's been years since I worked for this man, but I loved his son. And, as a remembrance to myself, I'd like to have this picture." The auctioneer gave her the picture and she went home with it.

In her old shack, she decided to put the photo on her wall, and as she pressed it to the wall to see how it would look, she noticed that something was between the picture and the cardboard backing. There was a little bump. So, she pulled the cardboard off, and on the backside of the photo was the will of the rich man. It simply said, "Whoever holds the face of my son dear, I bequeath all my possessions to."

This simple story relates well to our God. When we hold the face of His Son dear in our lives, God will give us more than we ever imagined – spiritually first, and then, physically and even financially as we apply His Word.

Do you know why I don't fall into temptation when it comes to drugs, alcohol and women, even though those three things were strong weaknesses in my life at one time? It is because I hold the face of Jesus dear.

Do You Love Jesus More Than Your Own Desire to Sin?

Some people will tell you how long they pray. They will tell you how much they believe and how much they love God, but they don't show it when the rubber meets the road. There has to come a time when you love Jesus more than you love sin. There has to come a time when you hold His face dear; when it's worth more to you than some sexual fling.

You may get saved and make Heaven your home when you die. But, you aren't going to get God's amazing possessions unless you are in love with Christ. When you love Him, you believe Him and when you believe Him, miracles happen.

When I got saved, I was a "long-haired hippy freak" that nobody really wanted. The church didn't know what to do with me. But, God promised me that if I loved Him, He'd honor me. He'd show me how to live. He'd bless me.

God never told me to cut my hair. I did that myself. He never told me to quit drinking either. I did that myself. He never told me to quit smoking dope either. When I found Christ, I didn't need the high anymore. I had the face of Jesus Christ and all the rest of that junk just clouded it up. I didn't want that. I wanted to see clearly and know the love of God for myself.

God is not interested in telling you all the things you have to do to clean yourself up – that's not His job. He is interested in opening your eyes to the deception of Satan so that you can live free. You may have many preconceived ideas about God, but they probably aren't even true. God is so much more than religion will tell you. His Word is powerful and He is available. The more you get to know Him, through His Word, and the more you reach out to Him, the more He will reach out to you and open your eyes to the truth.

"Father, Forgive Them, for They Know Not What They Do."

One of the most amazing things Jesus ever did was to show His love to the people who had just beat Him up and nailed Him to an old wooden cross. He was innocent but those people beat Him with a whip anyway. They punched Him, shoved a crown of thorns on His head and cut Him with a spear in His side. They spat at Him and made fun of Him. They were flat out cruel to Him. Yet He said this:

> Father, forgive them; for they know not what they do.

Luke 23:34

And, after that, they threw dice for His clothes! These were horrible people.

How many times has God nudged you to pray a prayer like Jesus prayed? Maybe someone did you wrong, and God was leading you to say, "God, they don't realize what they're doing." No! Most of the time we don't think like that.

When somebody does us wrong and God tries to tell us to pray for them we say, "Those devils from Hell! They know what they're doing, God! They aren't ignorant, they're just vicious and mean! God, kill'em…and let me watch!"

But, a religion without love is a religion without power. It fails amid the temptations and conflicts of life. A religion that is just made of hardness and hatred won't help anybody when they are going through the conflicts of life.

It's the love of God that we know in our heart that helps us to read the scriptures and believe them in faith. If we don't believe in His love, how can we believe in His Word? God is love! *"He that loveth not knoweth not God; for God is love"* (1 John 4:8).

God's Unfailing Love

Christianity's power lies in its recognition and continuation of God's unfailing love. He is a God of love, so, we as His children, should have love too. This doesn't mean we believe everything everybody says and should just allow sin to run rampant and say nothing. That's being foolish, not loving.

When somebody you know is falling into sin and you know about it, don't treat them like they've just gotten a contagious disease – like they're quarantined and off-limits to the Christian community. In times of trouble is when we should reach out to people – not pull away from them.

Whatever you do, when you know a friend is falling back, don't avoid them. Avoiding somebody who you know is falling back just drives them further away from God, and it's what the devil wants – to get them alone so that he can continue to wage war in their mind.

Being around encouraging people is what they really need – even if they don't realize it. Don't try and pin them down about what they've been doing or heap a bunch of condemnation on them for what you think they're doing! Even if you don't agree and can't stand the fact that the devil is stealing from them, don't start arguments and don't act self-righteous just because you're not sinning. When someone is going off course, this is the time to show the love of Christ.

You should never kick a person when they're down. It never helps anything. When people you know lose sight of their place in life and when they fall into sin, it's the time you should reach out and be a friend. Invite them to your house. Invite them to lunch or dinner. Even just a call here and there will let that person know that they're not alone and that somebody gives a flip about them. Just make sure that when you talk, you speak some good things.

Forgive and Forget?
Or Forgive and Wait for Fruit?

Not long ago I spoke with a preacher who had fallen into sexual sin. He didn't want to stop preaching the Gospel and began taking up the love message in the Bible, using it as a way to teach others how to forgive him completely and continue under his spiritual leadership. He tried to convince me too.

"We need to have the love of God in our lives," he said, "If someone commits a sin, we need to just forgive them and go on." It sounded good, but I could tell that the teaching wasn't in the right spirit. This was not about loving God with all his heart, soul and mind and loving his neighbor as himself – this was about hanging on to power. So, I posed a question to him.

I said, "Well, let me ask you something, brother. If you found out one of your ushers was stealing money when you received your morning tithe and offering, would you forgive him?"

He said, "Most definitely, Brother Jesse, without a shadow of doubt, forgive him. I'd do it instantly, immediately, because the love of God is that strong."

I asked, "Would you have him pick up the offering the next

Sunday?" He stopped talking suddenly. He didn't know what to say because, obviously, from the look on his face, he would never allow the man to touch an offering plate again! He surely wouldn't let him pick up the offering the very next week.

My point is that anyone can ask for forgiveness and God will forgive immediately, but the Bible instructs us that there must be "fruits" of repentance. That is something that takes time. So, God hasn't instructed us to live by the world's slogan of "forgive and forget" but to "forgive and wait for fruit." We're called to be wise.

Showing the "Fruit of Repentance" Tangible Evidence of Change

Just as it isn't wise for a preacher who falls into sexual sin to immediately resume teaching others, it isn't wise for you to leave your money around a former thief – even if he did repent. Don't feel bad and think that you're not being forgiving. It has nothing to do with forgiveness. It's about fruit, and according to Luke 3:8, that's something that the one who fell into sin is responsible to "bring forth."

You don't have to feel bad if you know someone else who has fallen into sin and you have a hard time trusting them. That's natural. You're waiting for their fruits to grow – tangible evidence that the change is real. You can love them, forgive them, pray for them and help them, but you don't have to trust them until the fruit sprouts! That's what I like to call "spiritualized common sense." The Word is practical!

Talk is not enough to regain a spiritual position like preaching;

talk is not enough to regain the trust of others no matter what job you hold. When a person sins and repents, it is the biblical course of action to start producing fruits – tangible evidence that change has, in fact, occurred.

If you're the Christian who has fallen into sin, you must realize that, even if you've repented in your heart, it may take a little time for others to reestablish trust in you. There is a time that you will have to prove yourself by your actions that you have really turned from those old ways and gone God's way.

If you're in the habit of going back and forth between living for God and living the old life, you just can't expect the whole world to believe you when you say, "I've rededicated my life to God again and I'm never going back to that old life!"

God forgives instantly and those around you may forgive you too. But, if you've burned them in the past with flip-flopping, you'll have to realize that they might be on guard. They don't know what you're going to do. So, this is the time to put some action behind those words and put some fruit on your tree!

A good tree cannot bring forth evil fruit, neither can a corrupt tree bring forth good fruit.
Wherefore by their fruits ye shall know them.

Matthew 7:18&20

Notice that the Bible also says, *"Bring forth therefore fruits worthy of repentance"* (Luke 3:8). You do the job of bringing it forth. It's not the job of others to draw it out of you; it's your job to bring it forth – show yourself changed. Don't just talk, do! Produce something that is in line with your repentance and don't expect everybody to give you back every ounce of trust that you lost the first week, because they won't. If they do, they're a fool and not even obeying the scripture.

Look, you may have changed through and through, but without fruit, it's just a wonderful story. Fruit is what makes it a real testimony that brings glory to God. So, you can't expect people to treat you as if you've never fallen – especially if it is something that included the breaking of trust. The Word instructs Christians to look for the fruits of repentance – the actions.

It's what you do over time that is going to regain other's confidence and trust. So, don't let the devil deceive you into thinking that people are "not walking in love" or "holding the past over your head" or "not forgiving" you. They just need to see some fruit on your tree. It won't happen overnight and that can be irritating, but let patience have its perfect work with other people.

Be patient. Since God was patient with you, exercise some patience with others. Don't let this proving time be a source of irritation. Instead, just take it one day at a time, knowing that, just as it takes time for fruit to grow on trees, it's going to take time for your actions to be recognized as true fruits of repentance.

Remember that nobody plants a tree and then goes outside the next day and picks an orange off the tree. Fruit takes time to grow. Over time, people will come to see that you're serious about living for God this time – that you've truly repented and turned from those old ways. As you live, day by day, just obeying God and being yourself, people will come to realize that there is nothing in Hell that you want anymore!

True Christianity is a Religion of Love

Christianity is supposed to be a religion of love that speaks the truth. If you haven't seen much love and truth coming out of the Christianity you know, then maybe you've been dealing with something other than pure Christianity.

What you have probably experienced is a mix of goodness and man's weakness. Don't ever blame God or dismiss Christianity based on what a Christian does! We're supposed to be known for the love we have for one another.

> *A new commandment I give unto you, That ye love one*
> *another; as I have loved you, that ye also love one another.*
> *By this shall all men know that ye are my disciples, if*
> *ye have love one to another.*

John 13:34-35

Jesus loved people. He cared for their souls enough to leave Heaven and give up all His heavenly privileges in order to come down here and die for you and me. His ministry was a faith-teaching ministry. He healed the sick and cast out devils. He loved people and taught them how to live, act and talk. Through His example, we learn how to live, act and talk too. *"Be imitators of God, therefore, as dearly loved children and live a life of love"* (Ephesians 5:1-2, NIV).

Work it Out, Day by Day

But, sometimes, we might mess up and don't live, act or talk right. I see people who aren't quite what they should be in terms of living for Jesus, but they love God in their heart. They really do. They mess up, but they've got a repentant heart and really want to do right. They're working their salvation out, day by day, trying to be the person God created them to be. That's how we all should be!

If I didn't have love working in my life, I might look at their mess-ups and say, "What is the matter with you, boy? You don't live right and you don't do what the Word says!" I'd be wrong to say that. I've found out that it's better to encourage somebody than to tear them down. If I just guide them with my words and give them some time to apply it, they'll grow on their own.

You see, Jesus' business was the business of reconciliation. That's what He came here to do – to reconcile us back to God. Once we get born again, our job is to follow after Jesus and help to lead others to reconciliation. That means we should tell people about God's plan of salvation.

> *For God so loved the world, that He gave His only begotten Son, that whosoever believeth in Him should not perish, but have everlasting life.*
> *For God sent not His Son into the world to condemn the world; but that the world through Him might be saved.*
>
> John 3:16-17

God's plan of salvation shows us the love of God. Sin will always take you further than you want to go, but God's love will always make you secure and complete. His love reconciles you and when you trust in it, it'll give you peace and joy.

Joyful Christianity

Some Christians never have fun. I have a knockdown drag-out good time in life! I flat enjoy myself! The only thing I don't do is sin. I don't want to sin. I enjoy clean living. I think that if you don't consider life fun without sinning, then the devil's got you brainwashed. He's stolen your ability to have any joy without him present.

True joy comes from the Lord. Life is an adventure, and the adventure is fun! It's not easy, but it has got joy all over it! God loves us and He wants the best for us – not the worst.

God expects you to accept His love, and start loving yourself too. I'm not talking about arrogance; I'm talking about being secure in His love.

People who aren't secure in God's love for them have a hard time loving themselves. They have a hard time being content with themselves or thinking good thoughts about themselves. I notice that they'll cut themselves down a lot. They hate the way they look, act and talk, but God loves His kids, no matter what!

If you feel this way, I've got some news for you: **God isn't inspecting you. He's inspecting the sacrifice.**

CHAPTER 20

God Isn't Inspecting You, He's Inspecting the Sacrifice

If you've struggled with guilt or shame over the temptations you've fallen for, I have to share a revelation I received from a friend that I believe will help to set you free.

The Bible tells us that, in the Old Testament, God's people brought their sacrifices to be placed on the altar to atone for their sins. The sacrifices they brought had to be pure and unblemished. They had to be the perfect specimen of whatever type of sacrifice they were bringing. They couldn't bring a sheep with a busted up leg! They couldn't bring a load of dented up vegetables with rotten spots. They had to bring their very best.

During this time, the church officials had an inspection system in place where priests would stand at the altars and inspect each sacrifice that was brought to ensure that it fit the criteria of being pure and without blemish.

Now, here's what I want you to notice – **the priests never checked out the people who were bringing the sacrifice**. If you were to have lived back then and brought your sacrifice to the altar, the priest would *not* have looked you up and down, checked in your ears for wax and checked to see if you had stains on your clothes. No, he wouldn't have inspected you at all. That priest would be interested in one thing and one thing only – the sacrifice.

Jesus is the Sacrifice

Who was Jesus? What did He do? What was His role on this
earth? JESUS is the Son of God – pure, holy and without the stain
of sin! JESUS is the Lamb slain before the foundation of the world.
JESUS went to the cross for the remission of *your* sin. JESUS was
and is and will always be your sacrifice to God.

So, who do you think God is inspecting now when He is looking
at you? He's inspecting the Sacrifice – JESUS! Once you are saved
and receive that cleansing blood, God no longer looks at you the
same way. Instead, He sees the blood of Jesus washing over you and
through you – making you perfect!

God is not inspecting you as a person, critiquing your every flaw
or fault. He has made a way for your sins to be eradicated and
washed away, never to be remembered against you anymore!

That's why I'm a happy man. Nobody is inspecting me – or at
least they shouldn't be! Jesus is my Sacrifice, my unblemished and
perfect specimen! So, that's why I can shout and quote, *"Let the
redeemed of the LORD say so, whom he hath redeemed from the
hand of the enemy!"* (Psalm 107:2). I have been redeemed! I can
easily say that I have been sanctified and cleansed *"with the washing of water by the word"* (Ephesians 5:26).

I can agree that I, *"being dead to sins, should live unto righteousness: by whose stripes ye were healed"* (1 Peter 2:24). I'm dead to
sin because Jesus is dead to sin! I'm living unto righteousness
because Jesus lived unto righteousness! I'm healed because of the
stripes from the whip that He took on his back for me! I can't do it
all on my own – but, with Jesus, I can! His blood is on me. It

covers me! It makes me able to rise up and say, "No devil in Hell is going to steal my joy, my peace or my life! Devil, get out of here because my Sacrifice has already paid the price for my sins and made me victorious over you! No weapon formed against me is going to prosper! I forbid it! I'm covered in the blood!"

Excuse Me, Devil!?

So, if the devil comes to pick on me, I just say, "Excuse me, devil!? Look at my Sacrifice. Let me ask you something. Where is yours?"

I don't have any, he'll say.

"Then, I can inspect you, you low-down, dirty dog, puppy from Hell!"

"I'm going to tell you what Jesus said!" I say, "Get thee hence for thou art an offense unto me!"

God looks through red to see my white hair. He looks through that sin-washing blood. Jesus says, "That is him. I washed him clean. They named him Jesse, which means wealthy, so I've got to make him wealthy too." Glory to God! I don't know about you, but I want to shout right now!

People have told me, "Brother Jesse, you seem so kind to people even when they've been in sin – and you know about it." "Well, I don't inspect them. We aren't called to be Inspector Cluso!" Jesus sits at the right hand of God. He is the Sacrifice who is always before Jehovah's eyes. That's why God sat down up there! There isn't any more to do right now. We have been cleaned through the Word of God!

Remember, God is not inspecting you for every flaw you've got – He sees you clean, pure and perfectly righteous because He's seeing through the blood of Jesus that has washed over you. He's inspecting the Sacrifice!

No More Guilt and Shame

Knowing that God is not inspecting you every second of the day will help you to avoid harboring feelings of guilt. God may convict you of your sin, and your heart will feel the "tapping" to do right, but when God convicts, it is not condemning.

God never says, "You low-down, dirty piece of trash! Repent!" No, what He says is more like this: "I love you, come back to Me. Turn away from those ways, and cleanse yourself in My Son's forgiving blood." He wants you to repent so that He can see you through the cleansing blood of Jesus and help you live a better life.

1 John 1:9 tells us, *"If we confess our sins, He is faithful and just to forgive us our sins, and to cleanse us from all unrighteousness."*

Once you say, "Forgive me, Jesus" there is nothing to feel guilty about. God doesn't see that sin anymore. It is "atoned" for; it is completely washed away from you and you're no longer held accountable for it. That is the grace of God – the power of the blood – and it is what makes you free!

Honoring The Blood

This great grace shouldn't be used as an excuse to keep on sinning. Galatians 5:13 (NASB) says, *"For you were called to freedom, brethren; only {do} not {turn} your freedom into an opportunity for the flesh, but through love serve one another."* There is an entire teaching on this in the book of Romans that further lets us know how to live by honoring the blood of Jesus.

What shall we say, then? Shall we go on sinning so that grace may increase?

By no means! We died to sin; how can we live in it any longer?

Or don't you know that all of us who were baptized into Christ Jesus were baptized into his death?

We were therefore buried with him through baptism into death in order that, just as Christ was raised from the dead through the glory of the Father, we too may live a new life.

If we have been united with him like this in his death, we will certainly also be united with him in his resurrection.

For we know that our old self was crucified with him so that the body of sin might be done away with, that we should no longer be slaves to sin—

because anyone who has died has been freed from sin.

Now if we died with Christ, we believe that we will also live with him.

For we know that since Christ was raised from the dead, he cannot die again; death no longer has mastery over him.

The death he died, he died to sin once for all; but the life he lives, he lives to God.

In the same way, count yourselves dead to sin but alive to God in Christ Jesus.

Therefore do not let sin reign in your mortal body so that you obey its evil desires.

Do not offer the parts of your body to sin, as

*instruments of wickedness, but rather offer yourselves
to God, as those who have been brought from death
to life; and offer the parts of your body to him as
instruments of righteousness.*

*For sin shall not be your master, because you are not
under law, but under grace.*

*What then? Shall we sin because we are not under
law but under grace? By no means!*

Romans 6:1-15, NIV

Don't be a user that perpetually takes advantage of God's goodness. Honor His blood, His precious sacrifice, and don't keep sinning without care just because you know God will always be there to forgive you. If you do, the Bible says that you are "frustrating" the grace of God. (See Galatians 2:21)

I've decided that I'm going to honor the blood of Jesus, and do what I can to live holy. If I mess up, He will forgive me. I'm assured of that. But, my heart is to do right, and I don't want to be the kind of person who abuses God's grace. Why? Because I love Him. I appreciate what He did for me, where He's brought me from and I want to show Him how much I love Him! I do that by obeying His commandments.

Titus 2:11 says that it was by the grace of God that I got saved, and it's also going to be by the grace of God that I say "no" to the devil.

Getting Love from Your Heart to Your Mind

Some people have a hard time with the concept of God's love, but I don't. I don't worry about all that – I just accept His love! God's love is like a gushing waterfall that is always being poured out upon mankind. You can't stop it from coming down! Once you're born again, that love starts flowing within you too.

Romans 5:5 says, *"...the love of God is shed abroad in our hearts by the Holy Ghost which is given unto us."*

The love of God is already in our hearts, but notice that scripture didn't say it's in our minds! We've got to believe in God's love with our minds too. You see, love may be in your heart, but your mind might still be filled with doubt, envy, pride and rudeness. It's your mind that you will strive to renew by reading the Word and allowing yourself to conform to its teachings. If you want a good idea of what real love is like, read this scripture!

> *Love suffers long and is kind; love does not envy;*
> *love does not parade itself, is not puffed up;*
> *does not behave rudely, does not seek its own, is not*
> *provoked, thinks no evil;*
> *does not rejoice in iniquity, but rejoices in the truth;*
> *bears all things, believes all things, hopes all things,*
> *endures all things.*
> *Love never fails.*
>
> 1 Corinthians 13:4-8, NKJV

Whew! That's the kind of love God has for you! Get secure in it so the devil can't play with your mind, and try to pass some of this kind of unconditional love along to others!

CHAPTER 21

Throwing Away Your Measuring Stick

Looks are so important to some people. Everywhere I go, people are always telling me I should dye my hair brown, but I could care less about that – God made this head and I like it. If I didn't like it, well that would be a different story. But, I like it and I'm not dying this hair now. I don't want to mess with that every couple of weeks. It's totally irrelevant to me.

My wife Cathy is always trying to get me to change my hairstyle too. I say, "I'm not changing it, woman! Leave me alone about it. I like it. It doesn't move after I spray it. I'm just going about my business and I ain't worried about the hair!"

Now, I have nothing against updating yourself if you want to do it. Do what you can to keep yourself looking good in your own eyes. Brush your teeth. Get some false teeth if you lose your own. Comb your hair however you think looks good to you. Lose some weight if you think you'll like your body better that way. But, whatever you do, know this, it won't change the amount of love God has for you. He'd love you if you were toothless, bald and never took a bath in your life!

Don't Believe the Devil, Believe in God's Love

If we don't believe God loves us, we'll eventually wonder if He cares about us. That doubt cripples our faith in Him, and faith is one of the components that we need to succeed in receiving all the promises of God. The other one is patience. We need faith and patience to get anything from God! So, when the devil tries to chip away at our knowledge of God's love, he's really just trying to steal your future. He wants to destroy your effectiveness in life.

When you know that you're God's kid and you are loved without measure, it changes the way you think in other areas. It frees your heart. You see, inside we all want to be loved. The devil knows this, and he'll try and chip away at your peace in this area if you let him. He'll try and beat you over the head with depressing thoughts that tell you you're not good enough to be loved.

God loves you, and knowing that will help you avoid falling prey to the devil's attacks on your mind about "measuring up." You don't have to say and do certain things in order to be loved. The devil will lie to you and tell you that you've got to earn not only God's love, but also the love of people. That's one he really harps on.

He'll lie to you and say that you'll be loved once you do this or that with yourself. He'll throw thoughts into your mind like, "If only you could lose more weight, somebody will love you" or "If only you had more hair, you'd be loveable" or "If only you had a better job, made more money, had a better personality, better clothes blah, blah, blah..."

All that pressure just to be loved – and you're already loved by the One who matters. God! He loved you enough to die for you and He likes you no matter what you look like, sound like or act like. You see, the devil is always looking for ways to cut you down and make you think you're not worth anything. He'll try anything to get you to inspect yourself.

Who told you that you've got to look a certain way to matter? God made you. He loves you. Of course, it would be good for you to be the best you can be so that you can enjoy life longer. But what is your personal best? You should make it your goal to be your best – not somebody else's idea of what your best ought to look like. Your security must come from God, and not your parts, because one day all of your parts are going to bite the dust!

Forget the Pressure of "Measuring Up"

Today, people are consumed with appearances and are always trying to measure up, but I think we should throw away the measuring stick. If you want to do something to improve your looks, it shouldn't be because society tells you that you are missing something. You should do it because you want it, and not because you feel some pressure to look a certain way.

Nowadays, looking good to the world goes way beyond dying your hair. Today, they can suck the fat out of your body, shoot stuff in your lips so they look like water balloons and laser off all your wrinkles! If your face falls, they can take the sagging skin and tie it all up behind your ears! You end up looking like you're standing in the wind, but nothing is sagging!

Some people hate plastic surgery and even go so far as to preach against it. I'm not against it. I figure that if you've got the money and want your eyebrows in the middle of your forehead – be my guest! Will God love you more? No! But, if it will make you happy, go ahead and do what you need to do.

If you had a tooth sticking out the roof of your mouth and hated it, you'd go to the dentist and tell him to pull it. So, if you hate your nose and want to get the joker lopped off, what's the difference in that and pulling a tooth?

Get your teeth straight if you don't like the way they look crooked. Lose some weight if it makes you feel good. Exercise, lift some weights – fix yourself up how you like. But don't think for a minute that it changes God's opinion of you, and don't think that you have to do it in order to conform to society's standards. Their standards change from decade to decade – so don't rely on them. Rely on God and do what you think will make you look and feel better.

I have to tell you, I've got some jowls on me that look like a hound dog! I don't like them, but I could care less if you don't. I can tuck this turkey neck in my shirt collar! Who knows? One day I could have these jowls whacked off and make my smile really go from ear to ear! When I say that, everybody goes, "No, Jesse! No!" But I don't care. I'll do what I want, not what somebody else wants. There isn't a scripture that says, "Thou shalt not cut off thine turkey neck" or "Thou shalt not fix thy teeth" or "Thou shalt not sucketh outeth thy fatteth!"

When I gain weight, it mainly goes to my sides and my face. The other day I looked at this hunk of fat on my side, got up off the sofa and went to get the vacuum cleaner. I was trying to suck that fat out, break it up a little – something!

But, I got to thinking, "I could put this body in tip-top, knockdown, drag-out shape and it still wouldn't be good enough to get into Heaven. It is too short and it is corruptible. But, God is going to make me incorruptible!" It made me want to shout right there in my living room. What a relief! Why feel that kind of pressure to measure up? In Heaven, we're all going to be living in incorruptible vessels – untouched by the effects of sin, sickness, disease, aging or death.

Get Rid of the World's Idea of "Perfect"

The world's idea of "perfect" is becoming more and more unattainable every day. Unless your life revolves around it, you won't make it to their idea of perfection.

The devil deceives many people into getting on the perfection treadmill. Don't be one of them. He will try and steal every stinking ounce of self-esteem you've got, if you let him. He'll try and make you feel like the ugliest person on the face of the earth. He's a liar and a thief. Kick him out of your mind.

Sure, you want others to think you're not a dog, but you've got to understand that there is more to you than meets the eye. Believe in yourself! If you don't respect yourself, respect the fact that God made you and He loves you.

You can't please the world. Some people are never going to like the way you look. They may have different ideas of what's good and what's bad looking on a person. So, don't bother trying to please other people. Please God instead by having faith in His Word and by communicating with Him every day.

All that you do to look better on the outside should be for your own personal pleasure and not to please the outside world or measure up to some "standard" of physical excellence. Whose standard is that anyway? The people who sell the wrinkle removing cream? The people who make clothes? That stuff is fine as long as you don't use it to try and "measure up." Throw away that measuring stick and be yourself.

Enjoy Your Life and Accept Who You Are

I've decided to try and enjoy myself a little. I'm done eating only broccoli and grains! Forget that! I'm having a little eggs and bacon every now and then. Fat or no fat, I'm eating my pecans!

I believe that we've got to stop judging ourselves so harshly and stop focusing on our flaws. We've got to enjoy life and accept ourselves and other people the way they are.

If a woman has some extra fat, why should she be treated any differently than a skinny woman? Does that make her less of a person? No way! Do a few less wrinkles around your eyes make you a better or more valuable person? No! It's ridiculous to judge yourself according to your looks.

I decided that if my flesh is dead, then I am like Paul – it is not me that lives but Christ that lives within me. So, I shouldn't care about some of that, because a dead man doesn't care what people think about him!

I've never gone to a funeral, walked up to the coffin and saw the dead guy pop his head up and say, "How do I look?" Have you? That dead guy doesn't care what he looks like? He could care less about what we think about him! So, why should you care what people think about you? I hope you understand the common sense and the spiritual concepts that I am trying to get through here!

Don't Covet Another Person's Parts

Coveting is a word we don't use much today, but it's in the Bible and was even one of the Ten Commandments. When the Bible says that we should not covet, it means that we shouldn't envy other people's stuff – and that includes body parts! People are bad about this, but I think women are worse because they're always feeling the pressure to look pretty.

But, a man can be walking down the aisle and see another guy walking towards him. That other guy might be muscle-bound like Mr. Universe. He might be dressed real good too. That man will look at the muscle-bound guy and think, *Look at that dude's legs! Look at the arms on that guy. I don't know how they build their muscles like that, but they just do it. I wish I was built like him!* If he's with his girlfriend or wife, he might even nudge her say, "Look at that guy over there."

The man is admiring the muscles, but he isn't coveting them. That's why he has no problem bringing it up to his girlfriend. He's just acknowledging that the guy looks good and that he is inspired by him. That man's thoughts usually drift to something else and you'll probably see him chowing down on a hamburger an hour later. His self-esteem won't usually plummet just because there is a guy in the room that is better looking than him.

Now, let me show you the difference between men and women!

If a woman is walking down the aisle and she sees another woman coming towards her that has a great figure, she won't react the same way. And, if the other woman is not only built great, but has a beautiful face too, it gets worse. A woman will rarely nudge her boyfriend or husband and say, "Look at that girl over there" or "Oh, look at that woman's figure! Isn't she just so beautiful?" They will steer your eyes away as soon as the girl comes into view!

And, if it's unavoidable for you to see her, they may narrow their eyes and telepathically try and tell the woman, "Don't you look at my husband. I will rip your eyes right out of your head!" Then, they'll start talking bad about the girl to you. They don't even know her, but they've got something to say!

They'll check her out from head to toe, cock their heads back and get irritated by her presence. They'll look her up and down and say something like, "What an ugly looking pair of shoes" or "Her dress is so tight, I could strike a match on her rear end!" They might say, "Just who does she think she is walking like that? This ain't the street corner, honey! Just look at her strut."

Do you know why they react like that? Maybe you know some men who react like that too. It's called fear of competition. It's about not being secure and not loving your own body. It's about wishing you had somebody else's body parts to such a degree that you actually resent them for looking nice. That's coveting and it's no good. It's a temptation you must resist if you want to be a loving and noble person.

Covetousness Will Cause You to Sacrifice Your Noble Nature

People who covet can't be happy with other people's success. They talk bad about people when they want what they've got. Or, they pick them apart and try and find a flaw so they'll feel better about themselves. A person can covet anything – from body parts, to jobs, cars, houses and even personality traits and spiritual gifting!

I don't covet anything. Why? Because if I covet, then I am sacrificing the noblest part of my nature – no one can harm me but me. You see, God made me to walk in the Spirit and to be at peace with myself. If I covet, then I'm harming myself because I'm continually saying that I'm not good enough. In fact, I'm a noble person because of what the blood of Jesus did for me. It made me part of the heavenly royal family – I'm God's adopted son! You are God's adopted child too.

When you're noble, you should have high moral character. You ought to be courageous, generous and live honorably. As God's child, you certainly are not meant to grovel and hope for better, because you're part of the highest ranking and most loving family there is. To covet is to sacrifice your noble nature. It mentally lowers you from the place God meant for you to be.

The devil is defeated in your life. He's rejected and restricted. But, if you let your flesh stand up and start coveting everybody else's stuff, you are just harming yourself because you are giving the devil a place to work.

Don't give the devil an opportunity to steal anything from you, especially not your security or joy. Kick that idiot out of your mind and build yourself up in the Word. Then, you will be able to resist the temptation to covet another person's body, job, house, family, ministry or whatever!

Today, I meet many people who are insecure about their lives. Because I'm around ministers so much, I hear some of them cut others down. They'll talk about another's ministry and say "I tell you one thing, I don't know how that guy ever got that!" I know that there is a spirit of competition there, which is just a branch off the tree of pride. There is a good chance they're coveting the other person's ministry and it's causing them to sacrifice their noble nature.

This isn't how anyone should be – minister or not. If you see another person doing well, don't gripe about it. Squash the fleshly need to cut them down. Be glad for them instead. If you go to somebody's home and it is beautiful, don't covet. Don't search for ways to steal from them or get into some jealousy, saying, "I've got something better than that!" Don't sacrifice your own noble nature for the sake of covetousness. Just be glad that God blessed them!

I Don't Have to Agree, I Just Have to Love

Personally, I've decided that I'm not going to covet. I'm going to love people, regardless of how they look or what they preach. I don't agree with all of the preachers I hear, but I love them all. I'll give you one better than that. I don't agree with everything *I* say!

As a minister, sometimes it happens that when you're preaching the Word under the anointing of God, something will just fly out of your spirit, go through your mouth and be a statement that leaves you in wonder. The words will still be hanging in the air while my mind starts thinking, *Hey, wait a minute...I don't believe that!*

Sometimes, God just has to bypass my mind. Maybe the point is a lot stronger than I can accept at the time, but I don't retract it or water it down with passive explanation. I just think, *OK, God. Help me out with that one. Increase my faith for it. I hope somebody here gets that.* That's what I think we should all do when we hear something that we know is right, but is hard to accept – especially when it's in God's Word!

CHAPTER 22

Loving One Another, The Difference Between Men and Women

There are some things in the Bible that don't make you smile and say, "I would love to do that!" Man, if I could rip out a few scriptures here and there and feel no guilt, I would do it!

"Brother Jesse, I would never do that! I love all the scriptures!" some may say.

"Oh yeah, what about that 'bless those that curse you' scripture? What about that 'pray for those that despitefully use you' scripture? Do you like being cussed and used?" No! Nobody likes that. Matthew 5:44 is one rarely used scripture!

If you get cussed out today, are you going to immediately stop, reach into your pocket and get some money out so you can "bless" the guy that just cussed you out?

When he goes, "You blankety, blank, blank, no-good blankety blank!" Do you say, "Haaaa! Let me give you twenty bucks! Here, let me bless you!"

If somebody despitefully uses you, are you going to pray for them? Let's say they lie to you, get close to you and pretend to be your good friend just so they can get understanding about your job – then they talk to your boss behind your back and apply for your job. You get fired. They get your job! Are you going to pray for them?

If you answered "yes" to either of those questions, I admire you! You're doing better than most Christians! Most people just don't want to react with kindness when they're being cursed! Most don't pray for people who use us. When somebody does stuff like that, most people's flesh just rises up! Most want to say, "Look here Jack! I will take this belt buckle off and stick it into your face! I'll tie the belt around the rest of your head and carry it home!" I've felt that way many times!

If somebody uses us, we want to say, "You no-good, lying devil from Hell! I want to break your legs for what you did to me, you low-down, dirty, piece of trash!" Then, we want to take them in the parking lot and whip the living daylights out of them!

We may want vengeance, but we're called to love.

Notice that I didn't say we're called to *like*, I said we're called to *love*.

Loving Prickly People

There are some people I don't like. They aren't just thorns in my flesh, they're complete bushes! They stick me every time I'm in close proximity to them.

Do I like those prickly people? Not really. Do I love them? Yeah, I do. I don't hold unforgiveness in my heart towards them because it would just tear me up. I may not understand why they do the things they do or why they talk so bad about me, but I make a concentrated effort to release them and not hold their actions against them.

Sometimes I mess up and say something I shouldn't, but I work on it and try my best to do right. I don't allow the root of bitterness to take hold in my heart. I forgive them, and I choose to pray for them and love them – even if I don't like what they do or say.

It takes time to grow. It's like the fruit of repentance I mentioned earlier. Walking it out isn't easy and nothing happens overnight. But, as you continue to read the Word and fellowship with Jesus, more of His love spreads around in your heart and you'll find it easier and easier to pass that love on.

Women Are the Most Amazing Creatures God Ever Made

One person you should make sure to love is your spouse. Women are the most amazing creations God ever made. My wife has got talents that you wouldn't believe. No, she doesn't sing and she doesn't tap dance either. But, the woman has got talents of her own that are hard to match. Take her toes for instance.

The other day I was putting on some shoes, preparing to go out and jog and one of my socks was further away than I could reach, but it was within Cathy's reach. I said, "Cathy give me that sock." Foom! The woman threw down her leg and clamped that sock between her toes and threw the sock at me! I looked at her and then got a quarter out of my pocket.

"Okay. See if you can get that, mama."

She picked that quarter up with those toes, and I started laughing in amazement. That woman has got some powerful toes! She's got hard toenails too. My wife has toenails that'll cut through steal, and she uses them to get me to do stuff I don't want to do.

I can sleep just about anywhere, on the floor, on a mattress, the sofa, a cot, I just don't care. I can even sleep standing up. I have had to do it in airports. At home, it doesn't matter if the light, the television or the radio is on. When it is time for me to sleep, I am down. A lot of times, I'll try and get into the bed real quick, before Cathy gets in. But, sometimes she's in before me, and even if I slip in real quick before she has time to tell me to do something, she'll still say, "You were the last one in, turn out the light."

"I can sleep with it on."

"Turn out the light."

Cathy can't sleep with that light on. It just runs her up a tree. I think it is funny. If I lay there too long, I'll hear her toenails coming across them sheets, "Shheewwwww." Those toenails will get me up in a nine-line second! That's like five little razors sliding across the sheets. I get up and cut the light off, Jack! That woman has got some toes on her!

Women are phenomenal! They are wonderful people, but don't make them mad. You could say something and not think anything about it, but they'll be thinking about it for a week. Argue with them and you'll hear a history lesson of everything you ever did wrong. A man doesn't have to worry about remembering anything. If he's got a wife, she'll remember and remind him of everything he needs to know.

Never Lose Your Sense of Humor – Especially if You're Married!

If you're married, you've got to learn to get along. One way is to show love to one another and to never leave your sense of humor outside. Bring that humor inside your house because if you live with anybody for very long, you're going to need it!

The Bible gives you some clues on how to treat each other in Ephesians chapter five. For women, it says to honor your husband and submit to his authority as the leader of your household. It says to respect him. Men need respect. It's a built-in need, so recognize that if you're a woman, and don't criticize and cut him down. It just tears a man down to hear everything he is not – and it won't get you any more love, that's for sure!

Love is what the Bible says women need the most. It's what the Bible tells husbands to do. Men should love their wives so much, the Bible says, that they'd lay down their life for her. It tells men to love their wives like they love their own bodies – that they nourish, cherish and protect their wives just like they would their own bodies.

A woman can live on her own and take care of everything, so can a man. But, together, they're a lot better off. Each one's weaknesses is usually the other one's strength. Women are stronger in some areas and men are stronger in others. There is no "better" gender, there is only different strengths.

Men - Love, Cherish and Protect

Because the Bible says that a man should love, cherish and protect his wife, you'll notice that women respond to that more than anything. Women are very affectionate. They want love to be shown to them regularly.

My wife used to want to kiss me before I went to mow the lawn.

I'd say, "Woman, I'm just going out there to cut the grass. What do you need a kiss for?" That was the wrong thing to say. It hurt her feelings because she wanted affection – small doses throughout the day.

Now, I didn't need that, so I assumed she didn't either, but I was wrong. Women like those little kisses goodbye, pats on the back and stuff like that. It is amazing!

If you're a husband and you never do that kind of stuff, you've got trouble coming. Here are a few tips for those of you men who don't know: You don't give your wife an appliance for Christmas. If you are doing that, quit! They may be nice about it, but that's a "house" gift. A woman wants something personal. The more creative you are the better, but if you're not creative, jewelry always works. Get the real stuff. You don't want your woman's hand turning green on you.

Flowers don't hurt either, even though they're as traditional as it comes. I have no idea why women like flowers so much, but they do. Get out your wallet and spend the bucks for some flowers every now and then. I know that they rot in a week and cost a fortune, but just do it. You'll be glad you did.

If a woman works real hard on dinner, don't take a bite and say, "Man, this tastes like trash!" I don't care if it does taste like trash, just eat it and smile. You don't have to lie and say it's the most delicious meal she's ever cooked, but think of something nice to say. If she worked hard, be especially nice about it. How would you like to work for a couple of hours in the yard or something, and your wife come out and say, "This yard looks like it's been mowed by a retard! Look at those ruts in the grass! Did you even see that weed the size of our house or what?!"

Women are sensitive. That is why so many women followed Jesus. As you research, you'll notice that it has been women who have kept the fires alive throughout the history of Christianity. So, treat your wife with love and sensitivity. Be kind to them and you can't go wrong.

The temptation is to disregard the woman's feelings. Colossians 3:19 tells us this: *"Husbands, love your wives, and be not bitter against them."* It's easy to get bitter at them, but the Word says resist the temptation to get irritated with them, shut down and ignore them. We're supposed to get involved with them and share their interests. Our job is to love, cherish and protect.

My wife, Cathy, has some interests I don't particularly care for – but I try to share in them sometimes because I know it's the right thing to do.

Women - Love, Honor & Respect

A man likes a woman who shares his interests too. I know Cathy doesn't really care about motorcycles much. She likes them, but she doesn't feel the way I do about them. But, she shares my interests, and it makes me feel good.

You see, a man wants to be loved and respected. As a woman, it can be tempting to tell your man everything you think about what he's doing wrong, but resist it! It doesn't help anything. Love him enough to respect his right to do things his way.

Respect your man's opinion and don't assume you know everything that is going on in his head – even if you do. You aren't his mother, you're his "helpmate." Is it really helpful to cut him down? Is it really helpful to make him feel like an idiot, even if he's acting like one!? Come on, ladies! Give us some respect!

Do you know what Proverbs 14:1 says about a foolish woman? *"Every wise woman buildeth her house: but the foolish plucketh it down with her hands."* Wise wives build their husbands up; foolish wives tear their husbands down. When you criticize your husband, it's like you're ripping out walls in your house. It just weakens the whole structure of marriage. Honoring and respecting helps to keep your household more secure.

Another element of a good relationship is submitting. Now, don't get nervous. It just means that a wife submits to the husband who is holding his place as the one who loves, cherishes and protects her in everything. (See 1 Peter 3:1-2)

You should submit out of reverence to God and because it makes you a good witness. Even if you think he acts like a idiot sometimes, try to obey the Word. Remember, we all make mistakes and act like idiots sometimes! Forgive the stupid stuff he does and don't hold it over his head. (See Colossians 3:13)

God doesn't want you to stay quiet all the time and not speak your mind. But you should try to say your peace in a loving way and not a condemning way. Bossing him around isn't respectful either. Nothing in the world is worse than a nagging woman who is always fighting and stirring up trouble in the house. Proverbs 21:9 has a funny scripture to think about the next time you want to nag him about something: *"It is better to dwell in a corner of the housetop, than with a brawling woman in a wide house."*

Don't get mad at me. I didn't say it! God did! You know, men don't need that much, but everything they do need falls into the categories of love, honor and respect. (See Ephesians 5:20-33) If your man works hard on something, compliment him. Praise never hurt anybody! A little "Good job, Charlie" never made anything worse.

So, recognize your husband's good traits and try to keep love and humor flowing in your marriage. Nothing breaks the tension like a good joke and laughter.

Women Are Running the World

I admit it. Most women are smarter than most men and can do more stuff at once! They are phenomenal creatures. They can work all day, come home and take care of their kids, run them all over town to baseball and dance classes, come home, cook dinner and wash clothes and still have time for talk to their best friend, their mother and their husband!

Man, the list goes on and on when it comes to what women can do! Their minds work on a different speed too. Man, if you're walking down the street with a woman, she could be talking about the world news one minute and see a pair of shoes in a store window that she likes and wham! She has completely switched gears on you! She has gone from talking about government programs to the new shoes out this season!

Women are running the world through commerce alone. If you go into a store, it's almost always geared towards women. The men's stuff is in the back somewhere by the bathroom. Check it out next time you're out. Why is it that way? Because women shop the most! So, those retailers know they must put the stuff woman like up front!

As a woman, I'm sure it can be pretty irritating to deal with a man when you think you know what is best. But resist! Resist! Resist! Resist the temptation to take over and tell him everything he should do. He is not you. He has different strengths and different abilities – and they're good.

Why This Stuff Matters

All this relationship teaching will help you if you're married and tempted by people other than your spouse. You see, if you stop doing the stuff that tears down a relationship and start focusing on making your own relationship better, you won't be so tempted by the prospect of another relationship.

If a man focuses on his wife and a wife focuses on her husband, both won't have time for anybody else! And, by using the methods I explained earlier in the book about combating thoughts with words, you'll just be that much better off in resisting temptation!

We're flesh beings, but we don't have to be ruled by it. It's OK to notice beauty. That's normal. You have two eyes, and if you see a good-looking person, how can you not notice that? Seeing beauty and admiring it is one thing, but letting your eyes linger on somebody other than your spouse and entertaining impure thoughts...well, that's another ballgame! It's not OK to lust – especially when it's not over the beauty of your own spouse!

Men Are On Drugs

Men have got a drug running through their body that makes them nuts. It's called testosterone and its working overtime in that man's body even when he's ninety years old.

For instance, if a good-looking young man walks by an old lady, she won't think much of it. She'll say, "What a nice looking young man" and keep going on her way. An old man could be stuck in a wheelchair and have drool running down his chin, but if a good-looking woman happens to pass him, he will almost fall over trying to turn his wheelchair around to get a good look! That's the truth! Men are on drugs! That testosterone is one heavy-duty drug!

But, no matter how much your hormones are raging through your body, God has made your spirit stronger than your body. You can tell that body to get down, and it will listen. Your body will always listen to your mind. God has given you a mind that has the built-in capability to force your body to get in line with the Word.

Your spirit always wants to do what's right, but your flesh (body) is weak. It just wants to do what's easy. But, what's best and what's easy isn't always the same thing and the battlefield is always going to be fought in the mind.

Some people go back and forth between what they think they can do. I find that it's best to make up your mind one time and say, "I can do this! I'm more than a conqueror! If God be for me, who can be against me? Am I going to let my body control me? Am I going to let these stinking thoughts control me? No way! I'm doing what's right!" After that initial decision, I think it's best to daily enforce your decision to live a pure life.

Deciding to live right is like brushing your teeth. Every day you get up in the morning and make the decision. Every day you talk to God. Every day you read the Word. Add preaching tapes and books like this one to your daily routine because they encourage you and give you some insight on how to succeed.

You can resist temptation and walk in love with others! God has made you more than able to do it!

Don't drink from an empty
religious cup

FILL yourself with

GOD

*so that **nothing else***

will fit

Being Full of God, Instead of Religion
Focusing on HIS Promises

CHAPTER 23

Empty Cups

Years ago when Jodi was a baby, my brother and I took each of our daughters to the beach. We ate a big breakfast before we left, and we enjoyed ourselves so much we never gave lunch a thought.

We forgot that kids are like puppies. You have to feed them a lot. At the very least, they need crackers or a snack to keep them going. Jodi noticed that Michelle had a little piece of bread in her mouth. She toddled over and took a bite – of the bread *and* Michelle's lip. Of course, Michelle started crying, and we felt bad because we hadn't stopped to feed them.

When you are hungry, you'll do whatever it takes to get food. It's instinctive. When you are hungry for God, you'll do whatever you can to spend time with Him. You'll get up earlier than you normally would, just to carve out some time to pray in the quietness of the morning. If you have a commute, you'll pop a preaching message into your car stereo system and fill your drive time with life. You'll make time for God because you'll feel like you have no other choice in the matter – you're hungry for Him and have to get your fix.

In His beatitudes, Jesus said that those who crave His righteousness would be blessed and filled! Matthew 5:6, *"Blessed are they which do hunger and thirst after righteousness: for they shall be filled."* In other words, you won't be disappointed. If you seek, you will find.

If you knock, the door will be opened to you. God will meet you right where you are, if you are hungry enough to go searching for more of His presence in your life.

Jesus always had people following His ministry because what He produced was life-giving and life-changing. His Words are in *your* Bible. Think about that. People traveled to hear Jesus, but you don't have to leave your house. If you want what He has to offer you – the power, the wisdom and the character to live well, it's available to you.

The Devil Can't Whip You

For years, people told me that I had to live in the ditch of life, that I couldn't have what Jesus says I can have. They told me the devil could whip me anytime he felt like it, but that was a lie – deception meant to steer me off course.

Jesus said that if you search for righteousness, you will be filled. I believe that it is the highest aim in life to become so full of God and His goodness that nothing else this world has to offer can fit inside your heart. With that much of God's goodness, you're going to have a hard time sinning.

Of course, the devil will try to convince you that you can't ever really live for God – not the way I'm teaching you in this book. That's another lie from the pit. You can do it. You don't have to be perfect, you just have to be motivated to seek after God with a child-like hunger.

The devil is empty of good ideas. A long time ago, I learned that I don't need to put on boxing gloves and go into the ring with the idiot. I'd have to take him out from under my feet to fight him. He's defeated already and that's why the Lord told us to simply resist him. *"Resist the devil, and he will flee from you"* (James 4:7).

Why aren't more people filled with the righteousness of God? I am convinced it is simply because religion has tried to kill the message of Jesus, the Person. They've sought to make you serve a dead religion, instead of a live Christ. You can't quench your thirst for righteousness by drinking from a sleek and satisfied religious "empty cup."

As a schoolboy, my friends used to ask, "What religion are you?" I'd say, "Pick one man, I've been there." My parents spent most of my childhood searching for God in various denominations. I grew up confused about the truth. I didn't know God. I knew religion – and that is man's tampering with God's purity.

There is a vast difference between religion and meeting Jesus. He is the Savior, not a jail-keeper. His desire is to free you, not put you in bondage – but that freedom starts in your heart when you open up to Him and let the chains of expectation fall to the ground.

Jesus will fill your cup with more than religious ideas; He will fill you with His righteousness and the presence of His Holy Spirit. The more you seek Him, the more He will fill you until you are "pressed down, shaken together and running over" (See Luke 6:38) with His goodness.

You'll, one day, look back and not even be able to recognize yourself anymore. You'll be so changed that the old things that used to cause you problems will be like water on a duck's back. They will roll right off. The very temptation that used to make you fall into sin will not have the least pull on your mind. That's what the Spirit of Christ can do, if you're hungry enough to go seeking.

The Unity of The Faith

You can't change anyone else. You can only focus on yourself. You may see all sorts of problems in the church and in the lives of other Christians. You can help and encourage, but you can't change a person's heart. Only God can do that for you, and only God can do that for them. So, don't harp on anyone who hasn't yet experienced the freedom of hungering and thirsting after righteousness.

God never said we were to come together in the unity of our ideas or our doctrines about Christianity. He said we were to come together in the unity of the faith, which is based on the sacrificial offering of Jesus Christ. Arguing over different interpretations of scripture is like drinking from an empty cup. It doesn't bring any refreshment and it only leaves you with an irritated mind!

You may believe the way I do or you may not. But, what's important is that we all believe that Jesus is the Son of God; that He was without sin, yet, He paid the penalty for our sin on the cross and that He died and was raised from the dead and is now seated at the right hand of Father God. This is the core of our faith, and it's what will unite us, regardless of what type of church we attend.

Will Jesus Find Righteousness or Continuing Sin?

Are you satisfied drinking from an empty cup? Or, are you ravenous for a real relationship with God? If Jesus made a trip to your house, what would He find? Would he find fellowship or would He find perpetual sin?

You can go to church every Sunday. You can read the Bible and pray. But, if your heart is not searching, you're not going to find much that you will actually apply. You can hear wonderful sermons on the blood, but if you're not thirsty, you won't apply it. So, you won't have the inner strength you need to conquer temptation and say, "No, there is nothing in Hell that I want!"

To live successfully, you have to drink from a full and overflowing cup, which starts flowing when you start seeking. The Word of God will produce faith in your life if you are "hearing and hearing" it. The more you seek God, the more valuable His Word will be to you.

God wants to fill you with His presence. He wants you to be a witness to others for Him; for others to see Jesus in you. Like I always say, the only Jesus some people may ever see is the Jesus in you or the Jesus in me. What is His presence but love, joy, peace, longsuffering, gentleness, goodness, faith, meekness and above all, temperance! (See Galatians 5:22-23)

> *And they that are Christ's have crucified the flesh with the affections and lusts.*
> *If we live in the Spirit, let us also walk in the Spirit.*
> *Let us not be desirous of vain glory, provoking one another, envying one another.*
>
> Galatians 5:24-26

When you live in the Spirit, you'll walk in the Spirit. In other words, people will see Christ in you. The demonstration that you show of His love and His power will not only make your life easier to live, but it will also quench other people's thirst for goodness.

Everywhere you go, the light of God that is within you will dispel the darkness that is around you. Jesus is the light of the world. So, if He's in you, then you will be a bright, shining light too. That's the power of His presence.

"I Was Going to Hell for Rejecting Jesus"

Before I got saved, I couldn't understand Cathy's need for the church or salvation. I said, "Cathy, you're a good person. You're a good girl. You don't drink. You don't smoke dope. You're good."

"Jesse," she said, "I wasn't going to Hell for any of those reasons and neither are you. I was going to Hell for rejecting Jesus." You see, no one is going to Hell for drinking, smoking dope, snorting cocaine or running around in immorality, because Jesus forgave those things before anybody ever committed them.

People go to Hell for rejecting Jesus as their personal Savior. That's the only reason anyone will go there.

If you've accepted Jesus as your Lord and Savior, you don't have the nature of the people in Hell. You don't fit in there. Hell isn't for you, and you know it. So, you do your best to walk clean and set your sights on living a good life too.

Colossians, chapter 3 says, *"Set your affection on things above, not on things on the earth"* (verse 2). Why aren't we to set our affections on earth? Because everything on earth is going to perish one day, but, until that day, we have to live and occupy our lives. Why not live with God's presence? Why not tap into His teaching and learn how to live joyful, peaceful, prosperous, healthy and free lives? That is what hungering and thirsting for God is all about. It's about tending to your spirit so that you have a good, earthly life.

Ministers Have to Stir Up Hunger Too

Hungering doesn't come automatically. It's something we decide
to do. Think about it like this. Have you ever gone on a diet, and,
suddenly, you're hungrier than you ever were before? That's the
power of the mind. It thinks, *"Famine! We gotta eat!"*

In the spirit realm, when you hold out on God, you start to suffer
the consequences. Instead of joy, you start feeling irritated and sad.
Instead of peace, you feel anxious. Instead of having patience,
you're hanging your fuse out the car window just waiting for
somebody to light it up! What your spirit is really saying is, *Famine!
We gotta eat!*

Have you ever gone on one of those diets that tell you to eat six
times a day? You think in the beginning that you'll never be able to
do it, but, soon, your body becomes conditioned and you start
craving a meal every few hours. Your spirit is similar.

The more time you spend with God, the more time you want to
spend with God and the more you recognize the consequences when
you don't. It's a lifestyle you develop that conditions your spirit to
grow and mature.

I want you to understand something, though. Ministers of the
Gospel don't have a supernatural infusion of spiritual hunger. We
are human. We have to stir up our own hunger and thirst. There are
times when we want to stay at home just as much as you do. There
have been times when I wanted to call some pastor where I was
scheduled to preach and say, "Put on a tape. I'm staying home."

But feelings have nothing to do with it. Not for me, and not for you. Tomorrow, when you wake up, you may not feel married, but if you've taken the vows, guess what? You're married. You may not feel like going to work, but you do.

We can't go by our feelings in any area of life. Are you one of those Christians who say, "The devil has been whipping me hard today. I don't know if I can make it this week."? If so, you won't make it. The devil's going to kick your head off unless you hook your faith to the Word of God that says, *"...he that endureth to the end shall be saved"* (Matthew 10:22).

Christianity is a lot more enjoyment than it is enduring. You might have to endure persecution, but you don't endure God. You enjoy Him. He's a blessing!

CHAPTER 24

His Promises and Our Performance

You're not serving a wimp God. He is the God who is More Than Enough. He never said, "I'll just meet your needs." He said, "I Am El Shaddai." He is more than you can even think. And, He can handle your needs, wants, dreams and your desires. He can handle your problems and give you the power to resist any temptation that comes your way. He is your "More Than Enough" God! You can depend on Him.

Too many people have been taught to approach God like this, "Most heavenly Father, don't beat me down. Please, don't whip me. I'm nothing but a low-down piece of trash. I'm just a low-down dirty dog."

No, you're not! You're the righteousness of God in Christ Jesus. He paid the highest price of all for you. He gave you dominion over all devils. He said, "Say to the mountain, 'Be thou removed,' not doubting in your heart. Believe those things you say shall come to pass, and you shall have whatsoever you say. Stay steadfast, immovable, abounding in the work of the Lord for your labor is not in vain. You're a chosen generation, a royal priesthood, a holy nation, a peculiar people. You are more than a conqueror. If God be for you who can be against you!?" (See Matt. 21:21-22; 1 Cor. 15-58; 1 Peter 2:9; Rom. 8:31-37)

That's what *God* said about you. All you have to do is believe Him and walk in the light of His words.

God Deals With Us According To His Promises

Yet, I've heard people say, "You know how God is. Sometimes He does, and sometimes He doesn't." That's an insult to the integrity of the Lord Jesus Christ. The Bible said you can ask *anything* of the Father. Which are you going to believe? Religion? Or God? Religion says, "Let's not get carried away with this. Let's ask for little." Those people are living on Christian bouillon cubes when they could be eating pot roast.

Why do some people expect so little of God? Because they expect Him to deal with them according to their performance. And, they know how they perform even if no one else knows. God doesn't deal with us according to our performance so much as He deals with us according to His promises. The blessings of God come when He finds someone who will seek to believe Him and obey Him. That's why He said, *"Blessed are those who hunger and thirst after righteousness, for they shall be filled"* (See Matt. 5:6).

I'm a blessed man, but, sometimes, my performance hasn't been good. I'll never forget when I started preaching. Those people had to endure. During my first message, sweat ran down the back of my legs. I prayed for the rapture all the way through that sermon. My performance was junk, but God didn't deal with me according to my performance. He dealt with me according to His promise. He said, "I put a call on your life, and you'll walk in the light of it."

I said, "Lord, I don't want to ever preach again." My mind agreed with the devil, *Let them go to Hell. They aren't going to get saved anyway.* My performance was severely lacking, but I was in good company.

Abraham's Promise and Abraham's Performance

Abraham's performance wasn't too good. God had told Abraham, "You're going to have a baby." He just failed to mention that it wouldn't happen until he was 100 and Sarah was 90. When Abraham finally figured out what the Lord had in mind he said, "Sarah's dead, and I'm a dead man myself." His performance wasn't up to par.

What about you? What would you do if a ninety-year-old woman in your church said, "I think I'm going to have a baby!" You'd laugh all the way out the door.

I met a man one time that looked to be about 59 years old, but he was 93. He still drove and traveled with his wife who was 90. I said, "What's the secret of your longevity?" I asked. He looked at me like I was some kind of a Bozo brain and said, "Haven't you ever read the 91st Psalm? You know, 'He that dwelleth in the secret place of the Most High shall abide in the shadow of the Almighty?'"

"Yes, Sir."

"I think you'd better read it again."

I decided to lighten things up with a joke. "Are you all planning on having any more babies?"

He looked me right in the face and said, "We're thinking about it." Then he walked out of the church. That man didn't just visit the secret place of the Most High from time to time. He dwelled there just like Abraham did.

God said, "Abraham, through Sarah shall the world be blessed."

'God,' Abraham asked, 'have you looked at Sarah lately?'
Sarah knew there was no way she was going to get pregnant at her

age. She told Abraham, 'Listen, we can't have any babies, because you're an old man and I'm an old woman. Take my servant, Hagar.'

'Okay, Sarah,' Abraham said. 'But I'm only doing this for you.'

That lying dog. He liked Hagar. He wanted her. After he'd gotten her pregnant, it caused a fight in the camp. Sarah said, 'Get her out of here!' Sarah would not have cared if Hagar and Ishmael died in the desert – as long as they were away from her and Abraham. But, that isn't God's way. Man's judgment is to kill and destroy. God chose to bless them both, but, through Isaac, He would bless the world."

Abraham's performance wasn't always right, but he was learning to add patience to his faith. He never had any trouble believing God, it was the waiting on the promise that got him in trouble. Abraham learned that faith will give you the manifestation, but patience will keep you going until it appears.

Obtain the Blessing

People are always asking me why I'm so blessed. I'll tell you why. It isn't because of my performance. It's because God looks in my heart and sees that I'm seeking Him. I'm hungry and thirsty for righteousness. When anyone seeks, obeys and believes, they will be blessed by God.

I'll never forget when I began to study the Word of God. I wanted to be a Greek and Hebrew scholar. There is absolutely nothing wrong with being a scholar, but, over the years, I've learned that there is a better way to read the Bible.

You need to read it in the Holy Ghost.

That's a lot more important than reading it in Greek or Hebrew.

Take tongues for instance. You can't speak in tongues apart from the Holy Ghost. I've had people ask me, "How do you speak in tongues?" I do it the same way you speak in English. I talk. God won't shake your throat, He'll simply give you utterance. You're the one who does the talking.

I can't speak unless I push air out of my lungs, over my vocal cords and move my tongue to speak English with a Cajun accent. I speak French and Spanish the same way. I have to push air out of my lungs, over my vocal cords and move my tongue – in any language.

A friend of mine wanted to be baptized in the Holy Ghost one time and I prayed for him until I was worn out. He was praying, "Give it to me! Give it to me!" Other people were praying, "Give it to him! Please give it to him, God. He's killing us!" That man had worn out nine sets of saints.

Finally, I'd had enough. I grabbed him and said, "You're going to be filled with the Holy Ghost tonight!"

"Do you think so?" he asked. "I came tarrying."

"Quit that tarrying stuff, you're wearing everybody out!" I said. I began to pray and the Spirit of God hit that boy. He sounded just like a Comanche Indian. "Hi yi yi hi ya...."

I thought, *That's not right!* But, the Holy Spirit spoke up on the inside of me and said, *"It's right."* Old boy got filled with the Holy Spirit with his eyes wide open. He stills speaks in an Indian dialect to this day. We were in a service once where some Indians heard him speaking their own language.

The Slow Road Sign Says "I've Seen It All. Nothing Excites Me"

Inevitably faith is lost when life's responsibilities slow you down to a quiet jog on an easy road. The less strenuously we seek after righteousness, the less strongly we believe in it.

I've heard people say, "I've seen it all. Nothing excites me."

That's a slow jog on an easy road.

I don't like people who are satisfied with that.

There are people all around them going to Hell, while they are just quietly jogging instead of running the race they were called to run and doing what God wants them to do.

Paul said, *"I press toward the mark for the prize of the high calling of God in Christ Jesus"* (Philippians 3:14). He was sixty years old when he said that and still going strong. The devil tried to kill him. People stoned him. He was drowned, starved, frozen and snake-bit. He just wouldn't quit.

Paul said, *"But none of these things move me, neither count I my life dear unto myself, so that I might finish my course with joy, and the ministry, which I have received of the Lord Jesus, to testify the gospel of the grace of God"* (Acts 20:24). When Paul had fulfilled his destiny, he said, *"I have fought a good fight, I have finished my course, I have kept the faith"* (2 Timothy 4:7).

"Running the race" is just a way of saying keep on going with God. Sure, it costs a lot to keep this ministry going. Sometimes I think, *Why don't I just quiet down to a jog along an easy road? There's no use killing myself.* Then, I remember. I'm not doing this for myself. I'm doing it for Jesus, the Messiah. He bore the cross so that the world might be saved. I will do my part. I will fulfill my destiny.

Set Your Thermostat

Your faith operates like a thermostat. When it's 96 degrees outside, the thermostat says, "Cool this building or cease to exist." The thermostat is set. It will not move. It will burn that unit up if it has to, but it will continue sending the signal, "Cool this place now!"

If you're facing cancer, diabetes or high blood pressure, set your thermostat to 1 Peter 2:24, *"By His stripes I am healed."* I'll tell you what will happen. You're going to start sweating. Why? Because the pressure and heat of life are going to come against you. But, that thermostat won't move unless you move it. Once it's set, don't touch it!

In the same way, set your faith for spiritual hunger on "ravenous." Don't be satisfied with an empty cup when God has prepared a banquet table for you. Go after the things of God with hunger!

You're Bored?

It's all a cliché.

Watch out

There is Danger
in "Familiarity"

Recognizing the Presence of CHRIST

Refusing to Act Like a Fool

CHAPTER 25

The Dangers of Familiarity

Years ago, you could tell the Pentecostal women by how ugly they were. They wore no makeup, long dresses, a bun and a face full of irritation! If a woman came through the doors of the church with makeup on and pants, the other woman would gasp for air and whisper, "Jezebel!" It was crazy. Everything was a sin to them, and even though the men didn't get to do much of anything fun either, the women definitely had it worse.

They were also blamed for everything that ever went wrong in a man's life. On top of that, they had to cover up as much skin as possible. They couldn't even wear a sleeveless shirt – and this was South Louisiana where heat and humidity made everybody sweat like a hog. I never understood why they couldn't show their armpits. I thought, *If an armpit turns you on, you need God!* There is nothing sexy about the pits, man, nothing at all. I guarantee you that a man never saw a woman walking on the street and told his friend, "Whoa! Did you see the armpits on that woman?!"

When I was a young boy, it got so bad in the church we attended that all people seemed to talk about was what others shouldn't be doing and wearing. They were so focused on the small, insignificant details of outward appearance that they forgot about the real, life-changing message of Christ. Christianity stopped being about Jesus, the Person, and started being about judgment and public opinion.

The Bible tells us, *"...for the LORD seeth not as man seeth; for man looketh on the outward appearance, but the LORD looketh on the heart"* (1 Samuel 16:7). It's natural to look at a person's exterior, but it's a better life if you try to see them through God's eyes.

Human nature wants to judge people by their outside appearance. It wants to say, "You're not this" or "You're not that." It seems like people enjoy dismissing one another, but it's dangerous to think you can know somebody by their looks. It's also dangerous to let yourself get so familiar with someone's personality that you stop seeing them as important.

Familiarity in Jesus' Hometown

Think about it. Who treats you worse than anyone else? Usually, it's your family! Why? Familiarity. They think they know you. They think that because they've been looking at you and talking to you for so long that you're not that important. A visitor may come to your house and get the royal treatment, but you? You get kicked to the curb! Why? Familiarity!

Jesus had the same problem. He left home, picked disciples and God started using Him greatly. He had built a good reputation preaching outside of his hometown, but it wasn't long before He went back home. The Bible says that it was the Sabbath and Jesus was scheduled to be in his hometown synagogue.

Now, I believe that Jesus probably was excited to be home. I'm sure He considered what He would say to the people. After all, these were people He knew personally, and I'm sure, He wanted to do well. Jesus preached and when He was done, the townspeople didn't give Him a standing ovation or a pat on the back. Instead, they gave Jesus one thing – attitude! They were angered and surprised to hear Jesus, a local boy, preaching with such wisdom and authority. They knew He'd been doing great things in other regions, but they resented Him for it…and they had no problem saying it to His face.

The Bible says, *"…and many hearing Him were astonished, saying, From whence hath this man these things? and what wisdom is this which is given unto Him, that even such mighty works are wrought by His hands?"* (Mark 6:2).

Why were the people so aggravated? Familiarity! Why did they question where Jesus got His wisdom and ability to do mighty works? Familiarity! They didn't have any respect for Jesus. They knew Him too well. They wanted to dismiss Him just like they dismissed everybody else they knew. It bothered them that He spoke with authority, and in fact, they questioned His worth as a man of God among themselves saying, *"Is not this the carpenter, the son of Mary, the brother of James, and Joses, and of Juda, and Simon? and are not His sisters here with us? And they were offended at him"* (Mark 6:3).

I don't doubt that this attitude bothered Jesus. I'm sure He wanted to teach the townspeople the truth and set them free, just as He'd done in other regions. I'm sure He *wanted* to share His wisdom and do great miracles. Instead, He sighed and said, ***"…A prophet is not without honor, but in His own country, and among His own kin, and in His own house"*** (Mark 6:4). The Bible goes on to say, *"And He could there do no mighty work, save that He laid his hands upon a few sick folk, and healed them. And He marveled because of their unbelief. And He went round about the villages, teaching"* (Mark 6:5-6).

Notice that it doesn't say that Jesus *wouldn't* do mighty works; it tells us He *couldn't* do any mighty works. Why? Familiarity. The people couldn't receive the Man God had sent, so they couldn't receive from God. Only a few people got blessed that day. What a shame. I'm sure there were people with serious needs that day, but they went home without anything. Why? Familiarity. They had become so familiar with Jesus that they didn't believe in His power.

When the Word Becomes "Just Words" to You

Today, in the church, people often become so familiar with the teachings of the Bible and the routine of religion that they no longer see Jesus for Who He really is either. They hear so much and practice so little that it becomes Christian cliché.

It's easy to get like the townspeople in Mark chapter six – all you have to do is think you know it all. But, that attitude stinks, and if you've got it, you might as well go on and sin with gusto because talking about the Bible but not doing what it says is just foolish. It's not just hypocritical, it makes for a miserable life too. Attitude is important and it's the lack of recognition for Jesus' real and life-changing power that will stop you from receiving what you really need in life.

You may have grown up in the church or you may have been saved for so long that it's become "familiar" to you – that can be good or bad. Familiarity can bring wisdom if you keep your attitude right and keep on believing God. But, the danger in being familiar with the things of God is that you can let yourself get so mentally accustomed to religion that you stop really recognizing Jesus Christ, the Person. This is one of the ways Satan deceives people in the church. This is why he fights your faith. He wants to degrade your thinking and render you powerless by ruining your attitude about Christianity.

If scripture has become cliché to you, watch out! There is danger in letting the powerful Word of God become just "words" to you. The danger is that you're living below your privileges as a child of God. If temptation comes, you're probably going to be a wimp. You won't have what you need inside to fight the devil off, and you're going to end up laying down like a whimpering dog.

Don't do that. If you've gotten lax, just pull yourself up and go to God in prayer. Repent and ask God to give you a greater revelation of His truth and how you can apply it to your life.

Remember that the Word isn't just a book of teaching, its words were inspired by a holy God. He is real and true, and His Word includes promises that will work for you if you will believe them. When His Word is real to you, watch out, devil! You are going to wipe the pavement with that boy! You are going to be able to resist the strongest temptation. You're going to use the Word and enforce his defeat. You are going to be someone that other people look to for support.

I like having an abundance of joy. I like having the ability to succeed. It's part of who I am because Jesus is living inside of me. I find that too many people fall into the thinking of Jesus Christ as just part of organized religion, but to me, Jesus is and always will be a Person! Jesus came to earth, died and rose again. He gave all those who call on His name the power to resist the devil, speak the Word with authority and live an abundant life – including me and you.

I preach abundance because it's what Jesus came to give us. If you've accepted Jesus, His spirit is with you and inside you now. Christianity represents Christ. It's not a series of doctrines to be adopted, a code of morals to be followed or a church to be joined. Christianity is a Person to be received, trusted and obeyed.

You can overcome anything this life throws your way, but if you let Christianity become so common to you that you stop recognizing its power as real, you're not going to be able to live the abundant life. Joy comes from God. Without a realization of His goodness, you're headed down a dangerous path. Life is going to keep beating you in the head and you'll ask yourself, "Why?" You see, if you want to have joy, Jesus has to be more to you than just a spiritual source that you praise in the church. He's got to become Who you turn to in dealing with the reality of daily life.

Familiarity can slowly drain the faith out of your heart. The devil would have you believe that God's Word is only good in the church, but that's a lie. It's good in your car, in your house and as you walk down the street. If you let the devil do it, he will steal, kill and destroy your hope by trying to convince you to keep those temptations your little secret. He'll try to convince you to keep those desires hidden away from God, as if that's possible! You can't hide anything from God, and when you repent, it isn't the first time He ever heard about it. Those secret things of the flesh that threaten to ruin your life are as visible to Him right now as if you just hollered the secret to your whole family.

God knows what's up with you. Hebrews 4:12-13 says, *"For the word of God is quick, and powerful, and sharper than any two-edged sword, piercing even to the dividing asunder of soul and spirit, and of the joints and marrow, and is a discerner of the thoughts and intents of the heart. Neither is there any creature that is not manifest in His sight: but all things are naked and opened unto the eyes of Him with whom we have to do."* God is not oblivious, but He has a way of doing things. He has given you a Bible to live by and it's His Word that is going to help you the most.

The Word is powerful and sharp and it can cut through those fleshly things, if you use it. That's why the devil works so hard to get you to stop believing. If he can cut your hope out, then he can dampen your faith. If you stop having faith, you won't do anything, after all, it is your faith and patience to keep on acting on the Word that brings results.

Christianity is a Person, Not a Religion

Keeping your relationship with Jesus alive inside *and* outside of the church is what is going to change your life – otherwise, you're going to struggle more than you need to. Why do that? Why beat yourself in the head all week long and feel guilty for falling over and over again? There's no point because Jesus is such a Friend, and He is available when you need Him.

Think about it. How much do you need Jesus when you're praising Him in church? Now, how much do you need Jesus when temptation is pressing on your chest and your mind is being bombarded with thoughts? You need Him more then, don't you?!

It's when the devil is attacking you with temptation that you need to pull on the strength of your Friend for help, and let me tell you something, Jesus is there. He's available. He can do mighty works in you and through you, but you've got to give Him the honor of recognizing Him in His hometown, so to speak. You've got to respect Him as your Savior – a Person who has much more to offer you than just religion.

When you bow your head for help in the midst of trouble, you are tapping into His power when you need it. If you wait until church to do it, you may pass up an opportunity to get stronger. You may give up the power you need for that day and end up doing something you wish you hadn't.

Life is about choices and the Christian life is about putting Christ in those choices. The more you say, "Hey, Jesus, I need your help" and the more you bring the teachings of the Bible into your regular, day-to-day life, the better off you'll be.

If you think living for God is hard, you're wrong. You're just not doing things right. You're making life harder than it needs to be. Really, it's all very simple, very black-and-white. Christianity is not about moral ethics. Morality is a by-product because Christianity is a Person, not a religion. People have gotten into Christianity and made it about religion. We've divided our faith into sects and formed our own doctrines, moral codes and churches. The truth is that there is only one church – the Church of the Lord Jesus Christ.

I guarantee that if Jesus was walking alongside of you, you wouldn't walk into another woman's bedroom and commit adultery. If Jesus was standing right next to you, I'm pretty sure that you wouldn't even let an adulterous thought lay around in your mind. And, if one popped up in your mind, you'd tell yourself "No!" and *immediately* cast it down. If an impulse to sin hit you, you wouldn't act on it. You'd *immediately* cast it down. Why? Because you would know that Jesus, the Person, is right there with you and you would want to keep yourself pure. It wouldn't be because of "Christianity, the moral code" or "Christianity, the doctrine." You'd resist because of "Christianity, the Person."

Before you can ever really resist temptation, you have to know Jesus, the Person, and recognize that He is the entire reason why you are saved. He is the reason you have any desire whatsoever to follow the Word or go to church. **He is the purpose behind the religion man has made.**

Jesus Had to Have a Sense of Humor

If there is no real Person behind the message, the harshness of religious ideas will choke the life out of you. But, I've learned that I can't judge Jesus by other people and what they do. He is fun. Jesus has a sense of humor. Just look at the crazy people He chose to run His ministry. He had to have a sense of humor with those boys on His staff.

Some of the people in Jesus' ministry were characters. Peter was intense! The boy would cuss you, cut you and then ask Jesus to pray for you! Was Peter perfect? No way. Peter was human, but the boy had tenacity, and he believed in Jesus, the Person. He repented easily too. One time, a rooster got him to repent. The bird cried out three times and Peter wept tears of repentance!

You know Peter betrayed Jesus, but, unlike Judas, Peter asked forgiveness. He let his sin be washed away, and he kept on with God. Sure, God had to work some things out of the man's life, but when it was all said and done, the Christian church was built on

Peter's work. That goes to show you that God can use anybody. He's not looking for perfection; He's looking for somebody to recognize their need for Jesus, the Person, and commit to keep on doing what needs to be done.

A "Don't Quit" Church

The early years of Christianity were filled with life, truth, healing, excitement and a "don't quit" attitude. The latter years should be the same way. Until Jesus comes back for His church, we should be flowing in the life He came to give us (John 10:10). But, there are some churches today that remain so regimented that if Jesus came to town to preach, I think they'd kick Him out for not fitting in with "the way we do things."

I believe that if Jesus would happen to get through an entire sermon, many church people today would probably smile to His face but never ask Him back! Why? Because Jesus taught and preached a real Gospel that was full of truth and life. He knew people would mess up, but He still preached righteousness. He knew people would fall, and so He preached repentance. He preached love, mercy and was constantly telling people to have faith in God.

Jesus didn't play religion; He hit the heart of matters with truth. Sometimes, the truth is hard for people to take. Truth makes you reflect on yourself. It doesn't let those dangers of familiarity hang around. It makes you stretch your faith.

Jesus wants to raise your standard of living and bring you to a higher level – not just intellectually, but spiritually, emotionally, and in a way that will transform the way you live everyday life. You don't have to play religion and "live" with what plagues your mind, will and emotions. I believe the Lord wants to reveal Himself to you and to show you, practically, how to stop being deceived.

Don't "Live" With It
Let God Help You Get Rid of It

You may have big things that you need Jesus to help you with. Maybe your whole family has a problem and you seem to have the same problem too. Guess what? You may be genetically linked up with your family, but you are spiritually linked up with Jesus Christ and that overrides the "family problem." You can get out of it and be the first one in your family to defeat that thing and live above it. I don't care if it's an addictive personality, sexual issues or a problem with rage. If you let Jesus help you in the fleshly area of life, you're going to live better than you ever thought you could.

Don't let anybody tell you that you have to "live with it" because it is "just the way you are." They may say that, but God says that you can do *all* things through Christ that strengthens you, not *some* things. (See Philippians 4:19) I don't care if you've fallen into the same pattern all your life. You aren't a wimp. You can break the pattern, and, besides, it's not your strength that is going to help you succeed anyway. It's Christ *in* you that gives you strength. But, you've got to honor Him enough to say, "I need you, Jesus. You're the One who is really going to help me make this change."

Stop feeding your weakness with words of defeat. Stop saying, "I can't" and start recognizing the weakness for what it is – a tempting measure from the devil to steal, kill and destroy your life. It's about deception. If you think of that problem as just a small, little weakness, you're deceiving yourself. Everything starts small.

If you consider it a problem that you can handle on your own, you're headed for a fall. That's just pride talking, and while there are some things that you can do on your own, you need God when it comes to temptations, tests and trials. You just need His help in order to succeed in resisting the devil and overcoming problems that have become strongholds in your life.

I'm Not Special – God Will Help You Too

It doesn't matter what level of temptation you're facing, God can help you. He helped me out of my old life, and if He did it for me, then He will do it for you. I'm not special by any means. I'm just like you – a person who needs God's help everyday and not just on Sunday. God delivered me from all sorts of trash living.

Sure, there are things I can do on my own because God created me with free will and I've got power over my own life. What I will and will not do is up to me. I can choose to do everything I can on my own if I want to, but when I choose to lean on Him for help, I'm able to rise to a much higher level. With God, I can break out of my own limitations. When I recognize that He is my Source, I can live above the problem instead of under the problem. I can succeed.

I live a better life with God because He gives me strength to overcome temptation and live right – and it's not a drag. As I said earlier, I know some Christians who are saved just enough to be miserable. Forget that, Jack! I'm living with joy. I have joy even in the midst of trouble, and it's not because I'm some "happy" person but because I've chosen to put my hope in Jesus. I honor His power and *choose* to receive from Him. That's how I'm able to have His peace when the circumstances say I should be living in my own anxiety. I bow my head to Him, honor Him and ask Him to help me with what I need. Then, I receive by thanking Him in advance for the help.

I'm confident, and it's not because I have some special ability or sense of self. It's because Jesus is powerful! When I praise Him and I release the pressures of life to Him, I can breathe easy. It makes living and doing what I do a whole lot easier. Sure, I could try to live this life all on my own, but I choose Christ because I know that not choosing Him is just plain stupid! He doesn't need anything I've got, but I need everything He has. Besides, I don't want to beat myself up trying to do what Christ has already made easy at the cross.

Don't Be Fooled by Jesus' Reputation

I attend church, not because I feel guilty if I don't, but because I want to hear what God is saying through others.

I believe that if you can't receive the Person God sent, then you're not going to receive much from God. His way is always through Jesus Christ, but God also has ordained people to help you mature and grow in the ways of God.

Ephesians 4:11-13 says, *"And He gave some, apostles; and some, prophets; and some, evangelists; and some, pastors and teachers; For the perfecting of the saints, for the work of the ministry, for the edifying of the body of Christ: Till we all come in the unity of the* faith, and of the knowledge of the Son of God, unto a perfect man, unto the measure of the stature of the fullness of Christ."

If you attend a church, you're not going to see a roomful of perfect people every Sunday. The people aren't perfect. The music won't be perfect. The pews and chairs won't be perfect. So, what makes you think that preacher has to be perfect? Unless Jesus descends from Heaven and decides to grace your pulpit this Sunday, guess what? You're going to be listening to an imperfect person preaching a perfect Gospel.

Your preacher doesn't have to fit your criteria of a "perfect" man of God. You may not even really like their personality. So what! They might not like you much either. Have you ever thought of that? People are people, and preachers are human beings, just like you. The only difference is that God has called them to deliver His Word to you. When you listen to them preach, you are submitting to the authority of their spiritual office. I believe that God wants you to receive from all the offices in His executive branch – the apostles, prophets, evangelists, pastors and teachers.

Some preachers you may like and others you may not, but when you don't listen to any of the people God sends your way, you may very well miss out on the wisdom you need to be more successful in this life. You need other people's perspective. If you didn't, God wouldn't have called people into the ministry to preach to you! We can learn from each other and grow stronger by receiving each other's gifts.

Don't get hung up on doctrine. You don't even have to believe exactly the same way as the person speaking in order to learn something good from them. Just accept what's good and spit out what's bad. God will lead and direct you.

Never let the devil deceive you into giving up Christ because of bad preachers or foolish Christians. People mess up and some just don't know what they're talking about! But remember that if it's just a preacher's personality that is annoying you, that's not enough to dismiss somebody. God has called all sorts of people into His work. Some of God's most fervent servants of His Word have been scholars *and* common, uneducated men. Some of His greatest workers have been philosophers *and* people considered by most to be next to fools! It takes all kinds.

That's why it's better to focus on making Jesus Christ your example. Let Him be the author and finisher of your faith. Remember, some people have done wrong things and given the church a bad reputation, but that's not Jesus' fault. He didn't fail you. He didn't fall. He didn't sin or hurt anyone by placing sickness, disease, poverty or anything else on people. When Jesus came, He healed. He miraculously provided for people.

Jesus wasn't a starry-eyed wimp. Sometimes people give that impression, but it couldn't be further from the truth. Read the Bible for yourself, and you'll see that Jesus was a strong man of God who calmed the seas, took authority over devils and spoke with unparalleled wisdom and power. He was anointed by God, and He loved people enough to help them out of the ditches of life. He did it by teaching and speaking the truth in love, by healing and doing mighty works. Jesus loved you enough to go to the cross and defeat the devil so that you could walk in His authority – today, tomorrow and for the rest of your life.

Don't Starve in the Midst of Plenty

Maybe you've been hearing the faith message for years and have grown bored. Maybe you've watched as Christians have fallen or your past experiences have caused your excitement to burn out. Maybe you have simply gotten accustomed to religious talk and have gotten into a routine of just talking and not doing. If so, it's not hard to change. You can start fresh with God right now. It just takes a decision to change your attitude, to let God soften your heart again, to be honest and repent.

Don't starve in the midst of plenty. Fill your spirit with good things and let the reality of His goodness flow out of you. Even if you think you've heard it all, Jesus can show you the exact part of the Word you need to understand more fully so that you can make the right choices in your life – the choices that are going to bring you the most joy.

For years, my daughter, Jodi, would ask me, "Daddy, how come you go to church so much?" I'd say, "I like to eat. I enjoy the Word of God." I've been in the ministry for many years and, yet, I've never gone hungry like so many preachers have. I've heard them talk about the misery of being dry, hungry and dead feeling, but it's hard for me to understand how it can happen. When you know Jesus, the Person, there is no going thirsty. He has given us living water that never runs dry.

In John 4:10, Jesus told the woman at the well, *"...If thou knewest the gift of God, and Who it is that saith to thee, Give me to drink; thou wouldest have asked of Him, and He would have given thee living water."* That's the point – if thou knewest! The more you get to know Jesus, and not religion, the more you are able to stop saying, "Well, I'll give this faith thing my best shot." Instead, you'll start quoting 2 Timothy 1:12 and declare, *"...I know Whom I have believed, and am persuaded that He is able to keep that which I have committed unto Him against that day."* He will be faithful to you.

CHAPTER 26

You're a King and a Priest, Don't Act Like a Fool!

Is it possible to be God's anointed and play the fool? In the Bible, there was a king named Saul who had a wonderful son named Jonathan. Saul didn't have the nature of his son. Jonathan wasn't trying to be the big dog on the block. Even though he had all rights to be king because of his family lineage, Jonathan recognized the anointing of God on another young man – David.

It takes more than just humility to give up a throne. It takes honor. And, to overcome any temptation, you need to develop your character to include a greater sense of honor. It's one of the traits that separates a fool from a king.

In the Bible, it says that after David killed Goliath, Jonathon honored David by giving him his robe, armor, sword, bow and belt – a sign that he was giving his authority to David so that he might become the next king. (See 1 Samuel 18:1-4) Jonathan put his own personal interests aside because, unlike his father, he had honor. He wasn't driven by power; Jonathan was superior to power. You sure won't find many people like that in the world!

King Saul's Pride and Fear

King Saul was in power, but instead of respecting himself and God, he let his power go to his head. Saul became prideful and began to fear the future. He didn't want to lose control, and he began to worry about how he looked in the eyes of others because he didn't want anything to change in his life.

Saul wasn't ready for the next phase of God's plan. He wasn't ready to give up his position, and, yet, God had already anointed David to be the next king. The people loved David because he defeated Goliath. David was an underdog and his victory caused people to praise his name in the streets.

The woman sang, *"Saul has slain his thousands, And David his ten thousands"* (1 Sam. 18:7). Now, that made old Saul flat hot! He said, *"...They have ascribed to David ten thousands, and to me they have ascribed only thousands. Now what more can he have but the kingdom?"* (1 Sam. 18:8). Suddenly, he was offended and his pride started turning to wrath.

You see, even though Saul was indebted to David for slaying the giant and winning the battle, it bothered him that David was getting glory so much that the Bible says he threw a spear at David the very next day as David was playing music in the palace! He said, *"I will pin David to the wall!"* (1 Sam. 18:11, AMP). Can you imagine? David is just playing the harp and, suddenly, he's dodging a spear.

And, that wasn't all. Soon, Saul couldn't take looking at David. So, he made him a captain over a thousand people so that he wouldn't be around the palace much. Then, he told David he could have his daughter, Merab, as a wife, but before the wedding could happen, Saul changed his mind and gave Merab to another. When another of his daughters, Michal, expressed her love for David, Saul agreed, thinking it would be good if David were "snared" by a woman. Saul wanted David to be distracted, to fail, to lose and to come to nothing, but that wasn't God's plan! It was the devil motivating Saul through jealousy.

The temptation you are facing today has a purpose too. It doesn't come out of nowhere. Temptation comes to distract you, to cause you to fail, to lose and to come to nothing. But, when you stick with God and decide to respect yourself, you can avoid the temptation by simply being smarter. In the Bible, it says that, time after time, David escaped Saul's attempts on his life. Why? Because David didn't let Saul get the best of him.

During these years, David chose to keep his eyes and ears open, to be wise and recognize that God was with him. God has given you the power to get wisdom from Him too. He has given you eyes and ears, common sense and spiritual strength. The closer you draw to Him, the stronger you'll become. God will be with you, just as He was with David during the years he was being hunted by Saul. And, just as David escaped Saul's attempts to steal his life, you will escape the devil's attempts to steal your life too. God is with you and you are never really alone or without help.

Why did Saul want David dead? Because he had two things ruling his life – pride and fear. Those two traits will get you into trouble. They're the marks of someone who is probably going to lose themselves to temptation. James 4:10 warns us to *"Humble yourselves in the sight of the Lord, and He shall lift you up."* Humbleness isn't thinking you are a low-down, dirty, piece of trash. It's about honoring God above yourself and His plan above your own plan.

Pride will cause even a wise man to fall. Pride will keep a good man from sharing his weakness with those who can help him to become stronger. Pride can keep a person from developing in Christ and recognizing the talents in others. Pride can make a king into nothing but a royal fool!

You see, Saul could have said "no" to the temptation to become angry and jealous. When he felt those first few stabs of jealousy towards David, he could have cast them down and reminded himself that God had used the young man to slay a giant and win a battle for the kingdom. Saul could have consulted God with a pure heart. He could have crucified his fleshly pride, chose to stop fearing the future and live out his reign with dignity. Of course, he didn't do that! And that's why we've got a perfect example now of what NOT to act like so that the devil doesn't rob us of God's best.

David's Honor and Saul's Repentance

Saul denied that he had a problem for many years. He didn't bow his knee to pray about the problem he was having. Instead, he just acted on impulse and ignored his growing weakness. In the end, Saul broke, and he repented. In his own words, he "played the fool" and "erred exceedingly."

Before he came to the place of repentance, he spent twenty years chasing David and came close to death at the hand of David. That's a lot of wasted time. And, why is it that Saul had to be killed almost twice before he'd release those feelings toward David and accept what God was going to do? Wouldn't it have been better if Saul would have learned before he hit rock bottom?

You see, wisdom tells you to get up out of the mud and start walking clean. Wisdom says "Stop going down the foolish road. Start acting like the king and priest that God has made you to be."

Saul may have been a royal King, but it wasn't until David spared his life the second time that Saul realized his great error.

It happened when Saul was asleep. He was again on the hunt for David, and he and his men were camped out. In the night, David and his right-hand man, Abishai, snuck into the tent. Abishai was so excited, thinking that David had the chance to make things right. He said, *"God has delivered your enemy into your hand this day. Now therefore, please, let me strike him at once with the spear, right to the earth; and I will not have to strike him a second time!"* (1 Samuel 26:8, NKJV).

Now, you'd think that David would have agreed since Saul had been a thorn in his flesh for so long. But, instead of agreeing and letting Abishai nail Saul to the floor, he defended Saul. David actually honored him and called Saul "God's anointed."

David honored him because he knew that, even though Saul was crazy with jealousy, at one time, he was anointed by God as king. Now, that's what a wise man does. He renders good for evil. This act shows you why God chose David to be the future king. David had the heart of a king even when he was squeezing pimples and tending sheep on the side of a mountain.

You see, it doesn't matter where you come from. If you humble yourself and develop the right heart and wisdom, God is going to lift you up. You are going to succeed.

In response to Abishai's suggestion that he kill Saul, David said, *"Do not destroy him; for who can stretch out his hand against the LORD'S anointed, and be guiltless? ...But please, take now the spear and the jug of water that are by his head, and let us go"* (1 Samuel 26:9, 11, NKJV). By taking those two items, David was proving a point to Saul – he could have taken his life, but he chose not to. This was the second time David spared Saul's life, and it had a profound affect on Saul when he awoke and realized what had happened.

The next morning, instead of going after David once again, Saul heard David's voice from afar off, and the bitterness and jealousy in his heart began to melt. He cried out to David with an entirely different tone as he asked, *"...Is that your voice, my son David? And David said, It is my voice, my lord, O king. And he said, Why does my lord thus pursue his servant? For what have I done, or what evil is in my hand?"* (1 Sam 26:17-18, NKJV).

David went on to plead with Saul not to attack him or kill him, and the more he spoke, the more Saul began to understand the great error he had made in judging David. As David reminded Saul that he respected his position as king of Israel, Saul hollered out a confession. *"I have sinned. Return, my son David. For I will harm you no more, because my life was precious in your eyes this day. Indeed I have played the fool and erred exceedingly"* (1 Samuel 26:21, NKJV). Saul repented, and that day, he stopped being a fool and started to, once again, act like a king.

Play the King or Play the Fool?

You are a king and a priest – even if you feel like a dog in the dirt at this very moment. But, unlike Saul who lived in the Old Testament times without a Savior, you have a position that is far above a political throne.

Jesus Christ gave Himself for you on the cross so that you could live as a king in this life – an honorable king – and that is a spiritual position endorsed by God and feared by the devil. When you use your authority and position in Christ, you increase in confidence.

The more you recognize your authority and position as a king, the more you'll be able to start acting with honor, overcoming temptations as they arise and walking in your divine privileges.

The Bible calls Jesus the King of kings and the Lord of lords, so, think about it. There must be kings that Jesus is King over – you are one of the kings that work beneath Jesus Christ. So, you don't have to shrink back thinking that you can't live a good and honorable life.

It's your rightful place to be a king and not a fool. You don't have to wait until you get to Heaven to start using the wisdom God gave you. You can use it right here and right now. God is El Shaddai, not El Cheapo. He came to give you life and that more abundantly (John 10:10).

I'm not some rinky-dink leader trying to tell people what they should and shouldn't do. It's God's job to judge and rule, but it's my job to be a king and a priest, to encourage others by living my life with wisdom, joy, holiness and honor. It's my job to not *be* a fool and to repent quickly if I happen to act like one for a minute! That's your job too. To *be* the man or woman of God that you've been made to be.

When you focus on *being* a king and priest, you will find yourself *doing* what a king and a priest should. You'll start acting on more of what you know is right and using a greater amount of godly wisdom.

When temptation hits you, sometimes you just have to ask yourself which role do you want to play? The Bible says that Jesus

"...hath made us kings and priests unto God and His Father; to Him be glory and dominion for ever and ever. Amen" (Rev. 1:6). That tells us it's a done deal.

You're a king, even if you are acting like a fool right now. Remember, Saul had every right to wear the crown. It was his destiny. He didn't have to act like a fool. He chose to. You don't have to act like a fool either. You can choose to be a king, to be a priest and to live wisely!

Be

the Person

YOU

were Created to Be

Strong

Vigilant

Sober

Settled

CHAPTER 27

Pretty Leaves on Rotten Trees

The first home that Cathy and I owned was in a town called Houma, Louisiana. It was a very small yellow wooden house, and it had a big, beautiful oak tree straddling the property line. It was huge – 114 inches around the base of the trunk, as I remember. It was a major tree!

In South Louisiana, we often have tropical storms and hurricanes. After we moved in, a minor hurricane blew through Houma, and during the storm, the wind knocked one of the big branches off of my oak tree. When I went out to look at the damage, I noticed that although the branch was huge, there was a hole inside of it. So, I called a tree surgeon to come and take a look at the tree.

He came and examined the tree, and said, "Mister, you are going to have to cut this tree down. If another storm like that comes, it's going to knock it down and you don't want it falling on your house. The tree is all rotten inside."

"But look at all the green leaves," I said.

"It is living off the bark. It is living off just the refreshment of the outer skin. But, it is full of ants and they've been boring holes in it."

"Oh, come on, man!" I said, "Are you sure?" I didn't really believe him. I figured he was just blowing smoke at me – lying to me so he could get the job to cut the tree down and make some money.

"Well, you can do what you want, Mister. I am in this business.

You want me to cut it down?" I really didn't want to cut the tree down because the tree was so pretty. So, I didn't.

About four months later we had a little thunderstorm come through town. There were gusts of wind and wouldn't you know it? Pow! Another limb cracked off and fell into the yard. I looked at the limb, and sure enough, it had a giant hole in its center too. I called the same man.

"I want you to cut this tree down," I said to him over the phone. So, a crew of guys came out to the house, and they began to cut the oak tree down in sections. It was too big to cut any other way without the risk of it falling on my house or my neighbor's house. Well, they began to cut and cut and cut until they got to the base of the trunk. When I looked inside the tree, I was amazed. There were only a few inches of wood in some places! The tree was almost hollow! I will never forget looking into that giant tree and seeing so much of nothing! Those bugs had eaten a feast of wood over the years!

"It is a miracle of God this thing didn't fall on your house and crush you," the tree surgeon said, "That's a lot of weight, even if the inside is eaten up." I nodded and we talked for a bit longer. They had to grind the stump down so the ground would be even. My yard was full of giant hunks of wood and saw dust.

The kids around the neighborhood thought it was great. They had a blast playing around the giant limbs and hunks of wood. It was a sad day to me, losing that big, beautiful oak tree – but it taught me a lesson.

A tree may be hollow and, yet, appear strong and beautiful. A person may be uttering fine words and, yet, be rotten at heart.

Fine Words, Rotten Heart

In Jesus' time, there were a bunch of religious people who had lost the meaning of their religion and were living a lie. They were the Pharisees, religious leaders who were much more politically minded than God-minded. They looked good on the outside, but inside, they were rotten.

The Pharisees walked around like proud peacocks, displaying their political power and daring anybody to cross them. Most of them didn't really care about living for God. They enjoyed the power of working for the church. Jesus called them hypocrites, snakes and vipers.

In Matthew 23, Jesus basically spends the whole chapter rebuking them. In verses 13 and 33, Jesus said they were children of Hell! Jesus flat couldn't stand their dishonesty and He didn't have a problem cutting those rotten trees down!

Some people think that because Jesus was so loving that He let everyone who sinned slide by without saying much about it, but that just isn't true. Jesus was a great forgiver, but He was outspoken about those who used His Father's Word deceptively. A sinner who didn't know much better was one thing. A religious leader who knew better, but decided to sin anyway, was another.

Jesus valued His Father's Word enough to stand up and say, 'Hey, you are doing wrong and if you don't change your ways, Hell is coming. Woe unto you, Pharisees! You bunch of lying hypocrites. You're gonna burn if you keep it up.' (My paraphrase of Matthew 23)

When Limbs Are Threatening to Fall

Do you know some people who are like those Pharisees in the Bible? Do you see limbs that are threatening to fall? If you see a man or woman threatening to fall, recognize that the devil has worked his deception in their life. But, although he may have eaten out their core, there is still hope for them because they know the truth. You may see God uproot them from their place of position – that's fine, let Him do it. Just pray for them.

When limbs fall, don't use it as an excuse to fall into temptation. Just because they lost out doesn't mean that you have to. You never want to be like the religious Pharisees. For your own happiness, you never want to lose sight of the heart of Christianity.

Remember, if something is chipping away at your core and you keep letting it happen, you are becoming a mere shell of what God wants you to be. Day by day, the devil's deception is stealing your strength. He'll keep chipping away at you until you're like the tree I mentioned earlier – pretty leaves, big branches, but nothing inside.

Check yourself regularly and make sure you don't get legalistic. Remember, you're not anybody's judge. Jesus could judge because He was God. But, we aren't God, and He will handle everything at the end. Our job is to keep a pure heart and live uprightly before God and do our best not to be a hypocrite. If the devil has deceived you, take your heart to the Great Physician, God, and let Him refresh you and fill your heart with new strength.

Sober, Vigilant, Strong, Settled and Perfect

The devil doesn't want you to live holy. He wants to steal, kill and destroy your life, to rob you of the blessing of living for God. Unlike God, the devil is a respecter of persons. He doesn't hit everyone the same. He wants to devour whomever he can, but he seems to focus on destroying those who he thinks will do something for God – even if it's just being a bright, shining light to those around you.

His aim is never just to hinder your life a little bit. **His goal is to stop you from being the person God created you to be – to make the Word of no effect in your life.**

> *Be sober, be vigilant; because your adversary the devil, as a roaring lion, walketh about, seeking whom he may devour:*
>
> *Whom resist stedfast in the faith, knowing that the same afflictions are accomplished in your brethren that are in the world.*
>
> *But the God of all grace, who hath called us unto His eternal glory by Christ Jesus, after that ye have suffered a while, make you perfect, establish, strengthen, and settle you.*
>
> 1 Peter 5:8-10

The devil is your adversary. The more you start seeing him as the deceptive and cunning demon that he is, the more you will able to stand strong when he puts out his bait. He wants you to fall. He wants you to lose. He wants to steal everything you've got in God.

Don't let him rob you. Resist! Be steadfast in your faith. That word "resist" means "to stand against" or to "oppose." It's a defensive action you take. You don't have to lie down and let the devil run all over you. Stand up against him, just like you would if somebody was trying to harm somebody you love. Oppose him and say, "No!" Your weapon is always the Word of God. When you speak up and use the Word, you are actively resisting him and letting him know that you can't be devoured.

Others Are Going Through It Too

You are not alone. God is with you, but there are also other people just like you who are being battered by the devil with the very same temptations. Let that be a comfort to you, *"... knowing that the same afflictions are accomplished in your brethren that are in the world"* (1 Peter 5:9).

Don't isolate yourself from others, if you're struggling with a particular temptation. Know that the devil and his demons are waging war on everyone, and if you share your heart with someone, you may find that they are having the very same problem too. Or, God may have already helped them through it and they may have some wisdom to share with you that will help you to be stronger. There is always more strength in numbers.

Remember that you are never going to be tempted with something you can't bear. After you've resisted and gone through the temptation, God promises to "make you perfect, establish, strengthen, and settle you."

God's plan is to bring you through it and establish you. The temptation you endure is actually going to strengthen your character. When you resist the devil, when you say "no" to the weakness, God turns right around and makes you stronger. Each time you resist, you become stronger and stronger. Each time you use the Word to combat thoughts and each time you display the love of God, you become stronger.

This Christian life isn't always easy, but it is better! We win! Don't listen to the devil's big roar. Don't let him take even a little nibble out of you. Shut that idiot's mouth by resisting. Be sober! Be vigilant! He's got to flee.

Dwelling in His Secret Place of Protection

God will protect you, if you stick with Him. Do you remember the story of Daniel and the Lion's Den? You are no less important to God than Daniel. He will protect you from every "roaring lion" in the spirit realm, just as He protected Daniel from those real lions so long ago.

How do you get His protection? By spending time with God in prayer and reading His Word. By making His Word the meditation of our heart. In essence, by dwelling in God's protective presence. Psalm 91:1 is a very familiar verse, but it means so much. *"He that dwelleth in the secret place of the most High shall abide under the shadow of the Almighty."*

The Amplified version of this same verse reads this way: *"He who dwells in the secret place of the most High shall remain stable and fixed under the shadow of the Almighty (whose power no foe can withstand)"* (Psalm 91:1, AMP). Now, those are shouting words! They tell you that you are protected! When you dwell in His secret place, you're in His shadow. Roaring lions can't touch you.

When Temptation Seems Overwhelming

When temptation seems too overwhelming to bear, take a look around to see if you're still covered in His shadow. Most of the time, when you feel you are losing the resisting battle, you'll find that you've stepped out of the protective shadow. You know, the Lord didn't say that those who visit the secret place get covered under the shadow of the Almighty. He says that those who *dwell* there are protected.

Remember that you serve a big God. He's not small or weak, and He can help you to make it through the toughest temptation. In His shadow, you're surrounded by Him. He is behind you, in front of you and all around you today. With Him covering you, you *"shall remain stable and fixed."* No temptation can overcome you.

There is nothing in this life that is worth swaying from God over. There is nothing in Hell that you want! It's a horrible, hot, teeth-gnashing and worm-infested place, and it's not the place you want to spend eternity. So, why live in Hell here on earth too?

Make a commitment today to live for God all the time, instead of just some of the time. Choose to be holy and pure before Him. You can do it! And, after this life is over, you move on to Heaven. Your rewards for living for God will be more than you can ever imagine. They'll be everything you want and more!

Heaven
or
Hell?

Which will **You** choose?

Your Destiny is Eternity in Heaven

CHAPTER 28

Hell is Not Your Final Destination, A Hellish Life is Not Your Destiny

It's not your destiny to be where the worm does not die and the fire is not quenched, where there is weeping and gnashing of teeth, misery and eternal separation from God.

It's also not your destiny to live a hellish existence here on this earth. God wants you to have joy and peace of mind and to be strong and healthy in every way.

If you don't know Jesus as your personal Lord and Savior, if you've read this book and, so far, you have not made a commitment to serve God, let me invite you, right now, to ask God for help.

You see, God has made a good plan for you through Jesus Christ. He gave His best when He gave His Son.

> *For God so loved the world, that He gave His only*
> *begotten Son, that whosoever believeth in Him should*
> *not perish, but have everlasting life.*
> *For God sent not His Son into the world to condemn the*
> *world; but that the world through Him might be saved.*
>
> John 3:16-17

Today, you've got a choice to make. Will you choose to believe and receive the truth, or will you reject God and push away His love? Heaven or Hell? Which will you choose? God will never force

Himself upon you. He loves you too much to make you do anything. He could, but He won't. He'll protect your choice to go to Heaven, just as He will protect your choice to make Hell your final home. Make no mistake, it's your decision and nobody can make it for you.

I believe that you have a heart that longs to know God in a better way. You may not understand everything, but you don't have to…all you have to do is reach out and He will extend His mercy to you. He will extend His love to you. He will use the precious and sacrificial blood of His son to blot out your sin and make you pure and holy in His sight.

God is holy and to approach Him, you have to be holy too. Sin won't make it to Heaven. It can't stand in the presence of such a holy and powerful God.

God is merciful and continuously extends His love to you. If you've been running away from Him, He is waiting for you to come to your senses and realize that being with Him is the right place to be – the only really good place to be. Sometimes God sends preachers like me to give reality checks to people who are so deceived by the devil that they actually believe that it doesn't matter.

God is merciful and patient, and He's doing all He can. But, unless you choose Him, you are headed down a dark road filled with all the entrapments of living in a sin-polluted world.

If You Want to Receive Jesus Christ...

Today, if you want to receive Jesus Christ, God's gift, all you have to do is pray to God and ask Him to come into your life.

Don't concern yourself with good deeds and bad deeds or with all your many flaws. Don't think about how "bad" you are or how you could have done better with your life. It doesn't matter. God knows and He loves you – no matter what you've done. He knows you're not perfect. He knows you've made mistakes. All He wants is to wash away those mistakes; for you to turn to Him so that He can help you live this life.

You need God's help. We all do. A new life will begin for you when you turn your life over to God, when you face your Maker and choose your destination – Heaven! Choosing God opens up a whole new way of living. This new life doesn't plop down on you from the outside. It's a life that starts inside your heart, the moment you turn to God and say, "I need you, God. I accept your ways and ask you to come into my life and change me." It's not just the words, but the sincerity of your heart that God responds to and it's so simple, a child can do it.

Maybe you are reading this book, and, no, you haven't backslidden into Hell, but you aren't living the way you should live and you want to make a fresh, new start with God. Don't be ashamed. God is here for you just like He is here for those who've never even heard His name. All you have to do is open your heart to Him. He will flood you with His presence the moment you recommit yourself to Him. Pray to Him now. Run to Him, and renew yourself in His presence!

But, if you've never been saved before and you want to know how to receive, read this verse. It is God's Word telling you exactly how salvation happens: *"That if you confess with your mouth, 'Jesus is Lord,' and believe in your heart that God raised him from the dead, you will be saved. For it is with your heart that you believe and are justified, and it is with your mouth that you confess and are saved"* (Romans 10:9-10).

Salvation occurs the very instant that you believe in your heart and confess with your mouth that Jesus is Lord; rededication happens the very same way. So, are you ready to pray? I've printed a prayer below that you can use as a guide. But, I encourage you to open up to God and share your heart too. God is waiting now and He will be faithful to hear you, wash all of your sin away and accept you into His holy family. Pray this prayer with me now:

"Lord Jesus, I ask You to come into my life. I believe that You are God's plan for my life. I need You in my life now. I want to be the person God created me to be. I don't want to be deceived anymore and I need Your help right now.

Jesus, I know that You are God's only Son, that You gave Yourself as a sacrifice for me. I believe that You died and rose again. Please come into my life right now. Change my heart, right now, as I say these words. I commit my soul into Your hands this day. You are now my Savior and my Lord.

I dedicate my life to You now, Jesus. I trust You because I know that You only have love for me. Thank You for caring about me. I accept You and know that, right now, You are saving me. In Your name I pray, Amen."

If you have just prayed this prayer, I want to congratulate you.

You are now in the family of God. Rejoice! Heaven is your final destination and all the blessings of knowing God and following His Word are now open to you.

You don't have to live a hellish life now that you are born into the family of God. You can now use the Bible's teachings and build a life worth living. You have access to God like you've never had before – right now. The Word of God is priceless. Don't take it for granted. It contains "God-breathed" teachings that will revolutionize your life.

I gave my life to God many years ago, and it has turned my life upside down. I'm known all around the world for my teeth! My smile! Why am I so happy? Because I have found the answer, and His name is Jesus Christ. You've just found Him too!

If I never get to meet you on earth, you can be sure that I will meet you face-to-face in Heaven. You might not recognize me. I'm going to be taller and with brown hair! I'm going to be sliding down the gold streets in my socks. I may pop my head in your window. I may be at your house every day.

It's going to be fun! Eternity with God! Eternity with Jesus! Heaven – there is no better place! I'm glad I'm going to be spending eternity with you. Until we meet, remember that God loves you with an undying love. He is your proud Father, full of admiration for you. Honor Him with your life, knowing that He will always stick by you. Be blessed and welcome to the family of God!

About the Author

Dr. Jesse Duplantis is a dynamic evangelist who has traveled throughout the world since 1978 preaching the Gospel of Jesus Christ. He is the founder of Jesse Duplantis Ministries (JDM), which has its International Headquarters in America and additional offices in the United Kingdom and Australia.

A best-selling author, Dr. Duplantis' books have been translated into thirteen languages, including Braille, and are impacting millions of lives all over the world. In addition, his television broadcast is reaching millions and can be seen on major networks in the USA such as ABC, NBC, CBS, TBN, Daystar and World Harvest Television. His program is also broadcast throughout Australia, Central America, South America, the Caribbean, Europe, the United Kingdom, Israel and the Middle East.

In 1997, he and his wife, the Reverend Cathy Duplantis, founded Covenant Church, a local outreach of JDM on the International Headquarters property in Destrehan, Louisiana, a suburb in the New Orleans area. In recognition of his many years of effectively sharing God's message of salvation through Jesus Christ to the world, Jesse Duplantis was awarded an honorary doctorate of divinity degree from Oral Roberts University in 1999.

Today, Dr. Duplantis is one of the most unique and beloved ministers of our generation. He has been sharing his memorable mix of strong, biblical preaching and hilarious life lessons for more than twenty-five years in thousands of churches and convention centers. Through world-wide television, video and audio tapes, CDs, books, magazines, the Internet, and revival meetings held across the globe, Dr. Duplantis reaches out with the Gospel in a way that captivates the lost and turns hardened hearts back to Jesus Christ.

Known throughout the world for his joy and his exuberant, evangelistic spirit, Jesse Duplantis is often told that he is "the only preacher my husband and kids will listen to!" Why is that? It's not just because "Jesse is funny," and it's not just because "Jesse is real." People listen because Dr. Jesse Duplantis is a true evangelist and revivalist. It's the anointing of Jesus Christ on the evangelist to reach the "unreachable," and it's the anointing of Jesus Christ on the revivalist to rekindle the fire in believers. People listen because they need the anointing of Jesus – and **Jesus is the message** that Jesse Duplantis preaches.

For more than twenty-five years now, Jesse Duplantis has had one vision, one goal and one mission – World Evangelism. He is committed to using every available tool to give everyone an opportunity to know the real Jesus.

Approachable, personable, compassionate and full of joy – that's the Jesus that Jesse Duplantis knows and loves. And, it's his mission in life to make sure that everyone on earth has the opportunity to know Jesus too.

What is Heaven Really Like?

Heaven isn't a place where everyone sits on fluffy clouds and plays a harp for eternity! It's a real and vibrant place that teems with love, peace, action, beauty and the amazing glory of Almighty God.

In this book, Jesse Duplantis shares several unusual events that have occurred in his life – events he likes to call "close encounters of the God kind" – including his testimony of being taken to Heaven in 1988.

Through these amazing accounts, your eyes will be opened to the power of God and the reality of life in Heaven. You'll discover the depth of compassion and love that God has for you, and be inspired to a closer and more intimate relationship with God as Jesse shares his *Close Encounters of the God Kind*.

Heaven: Close Encounters of the God Kind   By Jesse Duplantis
Book   BJ-02 $15

You and God...One-on-One Communication!

A God that we cannot see can seem very distant. Yet, He is closer than our spouse or dearest friend. He knows who we are, what our desires are, and our innermost thoughts. God is speaking. In *Wanting a God You Can Talk To*, Jesse Duplantis teaches us how to hear.

If you have wanted to get closer to God, then this is the book for you! Filled with practical examples from the Bible as well as Jesse's own experiences, Jesse will help you develop a closer relationship with God. Begin to talk to God today!

Wanting A God You Can Talk To   By Jesse Duplantis
Hardcover Book   BJ-06 $19

Look for these other books by Jesse Duplantis

Wanting a God You Can Talk To
Also available in Braille

Jambalaya for the Soul
Also available in Braille

Breaking the Power of Natural Law
Also available in Braille

God Is Not Enough, He's Too Much
Also available in Braille

Heaven: Close Encounters of the God Kind
Also available in Braille or Spanish

The Ministry of Cheerfulness

Jesse's Mini-books

Don't Be Affected by The World's Message

The Battle of Life

Running Toward Your Giant

Keep Your Foot on The Devil's Neck

One More Night With the Frogs

Leave It In The Hands of A Specialist

You can find these and other ministry materials by
Jesse Duplantis at www.jdm.org

361